Henry Athanasius Brann

Most Reverend John Hughes, first archbishop of New York

Henry Athanasius Brann

Most Reverend John Hughes, first archbishop of New York

ISBN/EAN: 9783743383586

Manufactured in Europe, USA, Canada, Australia, Japa

Cover: Foto ©Lupo / pixelio.de

Manufactured and distributed by brebook publishing software (www.brebook.com)

Henry Athanasius Brann

Most Reverend John Hughes, first archbishop of New York

"MAKERS OF AMERICA"

MOST REVEREND

JOHN HUGHES

First Archbishop of New York

BY

REV. HENRY A. BRANN, D.D.
RECTOR OF ST. AGNES' CHURCH

NEW YORK
DODD, MEAD AND COMPANY
1892

Copyright, 1892,
BY DODD, MEAD AND COMPANY.

All rights reserved.

University Press:
JOHN WILSON AND SON, CAMBRIDGE.

TO

THE MOST REVEREND

MICHAEL AUGUSTINE CORRIGAN, D.D.,

THE WORTHY SUCCESSOR OF THE GREAT
AMERICAN ARCHBISHOP,

This Work is Affectionately Dedicated.

PREFACE.

THE Psalmist tells us that the memory of the just shall never die. Archbishop HUGHES's memory should therefore ever survive; for he was certainly a just man, a faithful Christian, and a great patriot. The author has tried to show these qualities in this brief record of the prelate's deeds. But the author feels that he has drawn only a miniature, instead of a full-sized portrait of a great personality that filled the public eye for so many years in our city, State, and country. Still the features and character were so striking that even an imperfect picture will portray the man and the bishop. Those who desire to know fuller details and incidents of his life, can consult the large work of

Mr. Hassard, or the prelate's Complete Works, edited by Lawrence Kehoe.[1]

For many of the facts stated in this book, the author is indebted to these standard works, as well as to private sources. He hopes, in conclusion, that his readers after perusing these pages will have as much admiration as himself for the hero of his story.

---

[1] Hassard's "Life of Archbishop Hughes" is published by Appleton; Mr. Kehoe's compilation by the Catholic Publication Society, New York.

CONTENTS.

CHAPTER I.
His Birth and Early Education 13

CHAPTER II.
His Early Struggles in America. — Works as a Day-Labourer. — Enters Mount St. Mary's Seminary, and has his First Controversy 23

CHAPTER III.
He is ordained a Priest, becomes Rector of a Parish, and encounters the Trustee System in Philadelphia 32

CHAPTER IV.
His Interest in Irish Catholic Emancipation. — Controversy with Doctor Delancey. — His Letters to "The Protestant" 42

CHAPTER V.
The Breckenridge Controversy. — Father Hughes proposed for Bishop of Cincinnati 49

CHAPTER VI.

He is made Coadjutor to the Bishop of New York . 55

CHAPTER VII.

He goes to Europe. — His Interview with O'Connell. — His Great Controversy on the School Question. 65

CHAPTER VIII.

Close of the School Controversy 80

CHAPTER IX.

First Diocesan Synod of New York. — The Controversy with David Hale and the Trustees of St. Louis Church, Buffalo. — Bishop McCloskey appointed Coadjutor. — The Native American Excitement, and Mayor Harper 88

CHAPTER X.

He visits Europe in the Interest of Education. — His Political Opinions. — Organization of the Sisters of Charity in his Diocese. — Sympathy with the Irish Patriots of 1848. — His Controversy with "Kirwan" 100

CHAPTER XI.

He is made an Archbishop. — The Erection of New Sees. — The Know-Nothing Movement of 1854. — The first Provincial Council of New York. — Controversy with Erastus Brooks. — The Catholic Vote 112

CHAPTER XII.

His Hard Work from 1855 to 1858. — His Visit to Newfoundland. — Attacks on his Administration of the Diocese. — His Defence. — *Apologia pro vita Sua*. 127

CHAPTER XIII.

Archbishop Hughes as a Poet 141

CHAPTER XIV.

His Patriotism. — His Assistance to the Government during our Civil War. — His Mission to Europe to help the Cause of the United States. — Interview with Napoleon III. — Return to New York. — His Last Sermon. — The Draft-Riots. — His Speech to the Mob. — His Last Sickness and Death 154

JOHN HUGHES.

CHAPTER I.

HIS BIRTH AND EARLY EDUCATION.

IT is a common saying that "the child is father to the man;" and there is no doubt that the physical and social environment of youth has much to do with the formation of character and with the development of talent. This is especially the case of John Hughes, the great Catholic American patriot, who was the first archbishop of New York. The place, the time, the influences that surrounded his youth, helped to make him a strong character, a foe of oppression, and an ardent lover of American institutions.

He was born in the North of Ireland, in the County of Tyrone, in the little village of Annaloghan, on the 24th of June, 1797. His father was Patrick Hughes, and his mother Margaret McKenna. They were the parents of seven children, of whom John was the third. Patrick and his wife were typical Irish peasants of the eighteenth century, — poor, God-fearing, and industrious. Their neighbours were of different creeds, and as is usual in the province of Ulster, many of those who were Protestants belonged to the Orange secret societies, which were pledged to public and to private hostility to Roman Catholics. The penal laws against them were in full force; and bitter controversies were waged between the opposing factions. Some of the Catholics were no better than the Orangemen. The "Ribbonmen," a secret organization exclusively composed of so-called Catholics, were always ready to engage in physical conflict with the ever-belligerent Orange lodges. There was a fundamental difference, however, between the manner in which the clergy of the different denominations treated those secret societies; for while the Catholic priests denounced "the Ribbonmen," and tried to prevent their flocks from becoming affiliated to them, the Protestant clergy openly favoured the Orangemen, extolled them from the pulpit, as some of them still do, and were often members of the Orange lodges. This gave them great power in the North of Ireland, where they formed an English garrison. They were strongly in favour of maintaining the penal laws, which were not erased from the English statute-books until 1829. In that year O'Connell won Catholic emancipation. The reader may be able to judge of the influences surrounding young Hughes's life, by perusing some of the laws under which Irish Catholics were then living, and under some of which they still live in the ever-oppressed Island.

"No Catholic could settle a jointure on any Catholic wife, or charge his lands with any provision for his daughters, or dispose by will of his landed property."

"If the wife of a Catholic declared herself a Protestant, the law enabled her not only to compel her husband to give her a separate maintenance, but to transfer to her the custody and guardianship of all their children."

"If the eldest son of a Catholic father at any age, however young, declared himself a Protestant, he thereby made his father strict tenant for life, deprived the father of all power to sell or dispose of his estate; and such Protestant son became entitled to the absolute dominion and ownership of the estate."

"If any Catholic purchased for money any estate in land, any Protestant was empowered by law to take away that estate from the Catholic, and to enjoy it without paying one shilling of the purchase-money."

"If any Catholic had a horse worth more than five pounds, any Protestant tendering five pounds to the Catholic owner was by law entitled to take the horse, though worth fifty or one hundred pounds or more, and to keep it as his own."

"If any Catholic, being the owner of a horse worth more than five pounds, concealed his horse from any Protestant, the Catholic, for the crime of concealing his own horse, was liable to be punished by an imprisonment of three months, and a fine of three times the value of the horse, whatever that might be."

"If a Catholic kept school or taught any person, Protestant or Catholic, any species of literature or science, such teacher was for the crime of teaching punishable by law by banishment; and if he returned from banishment, he was subject to be hanged as a felon."

"If a Catholic, whether a child or adult, attended in Ireland a school kept by a Catholic, such Catholic, although a child in its early infancy, incurred a forfeiture of all its property, present or future."

These penal laws rendered "every Catholic incapable of holding a commission in the army or navy, or even to be a private soldier, unless he solemnly abjured his religion."

"The Catholic could hold no office or emolument in the State. He could not be a judge, grand-juror, sheriff, sale-sheriff, master in Chancery, barrister, attorney, agent, or solicitor, nor even a gamekeeper to a private gentleman. To teach the Catholic religion was a transportable felony; to convert a Protestant was a capital offence, punishable as an act of treason."

"To be a Catholic archbishop or bishop, or to exercise any ecclesiastical jurisdiction whatsoever in the Catholic Church in Ireland, was punishable by transportation; to return from such transportation was an act of high treason, punishable by being hanged, embowelled alive, and afterwards quartered."

At one time the government offered a reward of five pounds for the head of a Catholic priest.[1]

[1] "Memoir on Ireland, Native and Saxon," addressed to the Queen by Daniel O'Connell, A. D. 1843.

Such were some of the laws enacted by an English parliament after the breaking of the Treaty of Limerick; and although there was some relaxation of their rigour in 1775, when the American colonies revolted, and again in 1782, during the war between England and France, when a French fleet was in the English Channel and frightened the English government, the Catholic majority in Ireland had no rights which the Protestant minority felt bound to respect. This minority was chiefly made up of the children of the Scotch and English pauper emigrants whom James I. and later English sovereigns had imported into the province of Ulster, and settled on the confiscated lands of the exiled Catholic Chieftains O'Donnell and O'Neill.

Controversies between Catholics and Protestants were bitter and fierce around the home of young Hughes. Bloody faction fights between "Ribbonmen" and "Orangemen" were common; and in the contentions, treachery and assassination were more frequent than open warfare.

The archbishop used to tell that, when he was a boy, he was waylaid once by a band of "Orangemen," who pointed five bayonets at his breast, so that he thought his hour had come. However, when he told them his name, they let him go, saying, "We know his father." His father was a quiet man who, although a strong defender of his religion, would never associate with the "Ribbon" factions, the heads of which were often the paid spies of a government that fomented divisions among the Irish so as to govern them more easily. The "Orangemen" respected the Hughes family for their peaceable and inoffensive habits. He used also to tell, with bitterness, that when one of his sisters died, the priest was not allowed to enter the cemetery to bless the grave. The minister of the Catholic religion had to remain outside the gate of the graveyard, for a penal law forbade him to enter it. This incident deeply embittered the mind of young Hughes against the oppressor of his creed and country.

At an early age he was sent to a school in a place called Augher, and afterward to another in Auchnacloy near Annaloghan. He learned rapidly all that the elementary schools of that time and neighbourhood could teach; for he was passionately fond of books and study. He read the popular controversies of the day, and often listened to the oral controversies on religion which were then frequent in every town in the North of Ireland. Every village had its lay-theologian, its champion of Protestantism, and its champion of the old church. The faith of these theologians was often much stronger than their good works. Nor was the theology very orthodox or charitable on either side. In it epithets were often stronger than arguments. John was also fond of athletic sports. He had a strong constitution and a bright, lively disposition. In this respect, too, he was influenced by the physical surroundings of the time and place. The climate of Ireland is never very cold nor very hot, and although moist, it does not change suddenly. The Irish peasant of the period before the famine, ate plain wholesome food, and lived much in the open air. His food was oatmeal, milk, potatoes, and wheaten bread with fresh butter. Fresh meat was seldom used except on great occasions, as at Christmas, at Easter, or on the feast of Saint Patrick; even bacon and poultry were eaten only on Sunday. Irish luxuries went abroad to England, while only the necessaries of life remained at home.

With such diet, steady habits, and morality, the Irish peasants became the strongest race in Europe. The Irish soldiers who left Ireland after the Treaty of Limerick, were recognized as the finest body of men in the armies of the Continent. John Hughes, begotten of such chaste and vigorous stock, grew up amid such surroundings. He was a strong, sturdy boy, fond of work, fond of self-improvement, and fond of religion. He early showed an inclination to become a priest; but his parents were too poor to enable him to carry out his desire. Many a time when he was working on his father's little farm, he would throw down the rake or spade in the field, kneel behind a hay-stack, and, as he said himself, afterward "beg God and the Blessed Virgin to let me become a priest." He felt that he was called to something higher than farm-work. He felt the power of intellect throbbing in his brain, and the zeal of the apostle beating in his heart.

His father, too, saw that John would not succeed as a farmer, and therefore sought to get him a better place. This was soon found near Annaloghan, at Favor Royal, where the head-gardener of the Moutrays, a family of wealth, took John into service, and gave him lessons in horticulture, receiving the benefit of his labour as compensation. He also helped his father to till a small farm which he had leased at Dernaved; but he never gave up his purpose to become a priest. After working hard during the day at manual labour, he spent the evening trying to cultivate his mind by reading and study. The future archbishop, then a rough-looking boy, at the close of the day trying to learn Latin by the aid of a rush-light in a peasant's cottage, is a subject fit for the brush of a Rembrandt. But in Ireland it was impossible for him to realize his desire of acquiring a college education. The penal laws compelled Catholics to be ignorant, or forswear their creed. Their schools were prohibited. The Catholic farming-class was kept down, and systematically impoverished by absentee landlords, and despotic and cruel land-agents.[1] The

[1] The reader may gain a good knowledge of the condition of Ireland in these times from Carleton's "Tales of the

farmer who improved his land was punished by an increase of rent, demanded by an absentee landlord; and no matter what the economy of the tenant, he could never become owner of the soil. Patrick Hughes, like all of his class, felt keenly the injustice of these laws, which, by putting a tax and a penalty on the peasant's industry and thrift, rendered it impossible for him to improve his lot. His Catholic baptism made him a disfranchised serf, lower in the social scale than the Protestant pauper who was a charge on the county. Consequently the Hughes family longed to leave the land of bondage and seek the favoured shores of the New World. But it was not possible for all to leave at once. The father and the second son, Patrick, went to the United States in the year 1816, to prepare a home for the rest of the family. John left the service of Mr. Moutray, and returned home to help his brother Michael cultivate the farm. Patrick Hughes and his son Patrick settled in Pennsylvania, at Chambersburg, where they found work; and in the following year, 1817, John followed them, hating the government that had compelled him to leave his native land, and bearing with him a love for the land of his adoption, — a love that grew with his years and brightened his whole future career. Like all his exiled countrymen, he loved the

Irish Peasantry," and especially from his novel, "Valentine McClutchy, or the Irish Agent."

United States devotedly. Irish love of freedom is intensified by hatred of the oppression under which the people suffer at home; and consequently no foreigners become citizens of the United States with such eagerness and love of our institutions as Catholic Irishmen.

CHAPTER II.

HIS EARLY STRUGGLES IN AMERICA. — WORKS AS A DAY-LABOURER. — ENTERS MOUNT ST. MARY'S SEMINARY, AND HAS HIS FIRST CONTROVERSY.

JOHN HUGHES was twenty years old when he landed at Baltimore, in 1817. He thus describes his feelings as he crossed the stormy Atlantic : —

"I was afloat on the ocean, looking for a home and a country in which no stigma of inferiority would be impressed on my brow simply because I professed one creed or another."

For a time after landing he laboured on a plantation in Eastern Maryland, and then went to Chambersburg, in Pennsylvania, and worked with his father for over a year, doing all kinds of manual labour. In the following year his mother and the rest of the family, who had remained in Ireland, joined his father and himself at Chambersburg. Patrick Hughes, by labour and industry, was able to do in this country what he could not have done in Ireland, — he left his family a house and some land when he died, in 1837, at the age of seventy. Before his death he had the consolation of seeing John a priest.

John, when a young man of twenty, was usually reserved, always well-dressed and respectable, self-possessed and of quiet manners. He had a distinguished look even in his poverty. He was of a lively disposition, and could tell a good story and sing a good song. He was a member of the village choir. Every one looked on him as one destined to make his mark in a career above his actual station. He persevered in his studious habits, and in his purpose of entering the holy ministry. He had heard that about thirty miles from Chambersburg, among the hills of Emmittsburg, was the Seminary of Mount St. Mary,—an institution for the education of Catholics both lay and clerical. Into this institution poor students were often admitted, if they intended to become priests, and in return for their services as teachers in the college, they received the necessary training in theology.

John made several applications for admission, but repeatedly failed. When he called, he was often told that there was no vacancy; but he was determined not to miss his opportunity. He went to live at Emmittsburg, in order to be near the college. He worked in the town as a common labourer, and helped to dig a mill-race and build a stone bridge over a little stream running between Emmittsburg and

Taneytown. This bridge was often pointed out afterward as the scene of his early labours. He boarded with a schoolmaster named Mullen, one of his own countrymen. John's fellow-workmen recognized in him a superior, such was the natural dignity of his manner and the force even of his uncultured mind; the better classes of the neighbourhood treated him as an equal. With anxiety he watched the college, and prayed for the expected admission.

The president of this renowned institution was then the Rev. John Dubois, a French priest who afterward became bishop of New York. He had been a fellow-student in Paris with Robespierre, and had seen much of the horrors of the French Revolution. He came to this country with letters of recommendation from Lafayette, to some of the prominent Virginia families of the time, — such as the Lees and the Randolphs, — and to Patrick Henry. Dubois was a typical pioneer-priest of the best French type, — strong-willed, hard-working, zealous, and pious, easily accommodating himself to his surroundings, no matter how unpleasant. He founded Mount St. Mary's in spite of many difficulties, and made it for years the centre of Catholic education in our young republic.

In 1819, after various refusals, Mr. Hughes again made application to Father Dubois for admission to the seminary. He received the usual answer, — there was no vacancy; but a qualification was added:

"All I can do," said Father Dubois to the future archbishop of New York, "is to give you work in the garden." Mr. Hughes at once accepted the offer, and became superintendent of the college garden. In return for his services he was to receive board, lodging, and private instruction until he should be able to teach a class and be formally admitted among the levites of the seminary. It was November 10, 1819, when the dream of his boyish years in Ireland was about to be realized, and the harvest of his perseverance and fervent prayer was about to be reaped.

As all the students at Mount St. Mary's worked occasionally at manual labour in those days,—either for the sake of saving expense, or for their health,— Mr. Hughes's position as a gardener did not lower him in the eyes of the other students. He had under him the coloured men Timothy and Peter, who lived at the college for many years after he had left it. During the nine months he held this post, he used every spare moment in the prosecution of his studies. One day during the dinner-hour Father Dubois found him studying instead of eating his meal. This impressed the mind of the president, who began to question the industrious young man, and finding that he had made wonderful progress in Latin, relieved him of many of his duties in the garden and took him into the college as a regular student, in A. D. 1820. Father Dubois was a good judge of character, and recognized the force of his future coadjutor and successor in the See of New York.

Another French priest who then helped Father Dubois in the management of the college, was the saintly and learned Father Bruté, who afterward became the first bishop of Vincennes. He was born at Rennes, in Brittany, France, March 20, 1779, studied medicine in Paris, and after finishing his course, gave up the world and entered the Seminary of St. Sulpice, and was ordained a priest there in 1808. Five years later he came to the United States as a missionary, with another of his countrymen, Father Flaget, afterward the first bishop of Bardstown, Kentucky.

Although Mr. Hughes was at this time twenty-three years old, his memory was as good as that of the brightest of the college lads, and he made great progress in his studies under his able professor, Father Bruté. He learned rapidly while employed in teaching others. He gave instruction in the common English branches, and in the rudiments of Latin, to the lower classes in the college, and at the same time superintended the workmen in the garden. He was a rigid disciplinarian, and the unruly boys dreaded him. They felt that they were under a man born to command, and that he would compel them to obey by physical force if necessary. He was therefore an excellent prefect. The boys feared his sarcasm as much as they dreaded his physical strength. Some of them occasionally sought revenge for punishment by mocking his Irish accent and race. Once a party of boys, the leader of whom was the son of a well-known judge, made a stuffed figure to represent Saint Patrick; and on the 17th of March, the feast of the Saint, at a given signal they hoisted it and hung it to one of the rafters of the study hall, while Mr. Hughes was keeping order in the prefect's chair. He looked quietly at the figure, and then sharply at the ringleader of the unruly set, and said aloud: "O tempora, O mores! the son of a judge has become a hangman." There was a laugh at the culprit, and the name of "Jack Ketch" stuck to him afterward through his whole college career. The boys played no more tricks on the stalwart seminarian.

He soon had an opportunity of engaging in his first important religious controversy. It was the style in those days to attack the Catholic Church everywhere, and sometimes even in Fourth of July speeches. Some orator had made an attack on the Church on the Fourth of July, at Chambersburg, and Mr. Hughes was asked to reply. He did so; but so sharply that the editor of the "Franklin Repository" could hardly be prevailed on to publish his letter. He felt bitterly and keenly the false charges which were made against his creed, and he found it hard to show mercy to calumniators who ought to know, and who often did know, that they were stating falsehoods. He was still but an untrained writer and an undeveloped orator. When called upon to read his first essay before the college literary society, he broke down. He was so nervous that he could not open his mouth, and the paper fell from his hands. But he soon got over his timidity and became an able debater. His application to study was intense. An ordinary constitution would have broken down under the circumstances; but his blood was pure, the mountain air was good, and the healthful excursions which he made with the other students in long rambles, sometimes even as far as Chambersburg, where he often visited his parents, kept his body vigorous and gave the necessary recreation to his mind.

On one occasion a fire broke out in the woods near the college, and the whole faculty and the students were summoned to stem the advance of the flames. Such was the common respect for Mr. Hughes's ability, that he was unanimously chosen commander of the forces. All implicitly obeyed him, and in a short time the flames were conquered. Every one saw in him the courage of the soldier and the skill of the general. He planned, stationed sentinels along the fire-belt, hurried from place to place, ordering, encouraging the boys and the men, and working more than any one himself. When the fire was out, he retired from the field, late at night, with his best coat nearly burned off his back. As he was too poor to buy a new one, for months he wore the old one, with a large patch between his shoulders.

About the year 1823 he had acquired sufficient classical knowledge to entitle him to begin the study of theology. He was then twenty-six years of age; thus commencing his theological studies at an age when most seminarians have finished their course and have gone to their work as priests. His advanced age, however, had given him the experience and the ripeness of judgment so necessary to the American missionary, the early years of whose ministry are surrounded by so many temptations and dangers. The saintly and learned Father Bruté taught him theology. How delighted must the young seminarian have been when he first donned the cassock for which he had longed in childhood; and how his heart beat with pleasure as he felt the time for his ordination draw near. His mental powers developed rapidly under culture. He was fast gaining a reputation in the college as an orator, although his gestures were still far from graceful; but his diction was pure, and his emotional power great. He was always a writer of good English, and he had the talent of expressing his thoughts with clearness and force. The college boys feared and admired, while the professors respected him. He rose in the seminary and in the college. He was made chief-prefect of discipline.

But as he belonged to the old school, and believed that he who spared the rod spoiled the child, he often inflicted physical chastisement on the misbehaving boys. On this account he was soon removed from office by his superiors, who preferred a milder system of government.

In 1824 the college was burned down, and the seminarists went about the country collecting funds to build a new one. Mr. Hughes was very successful in his efforts among his old neighbours and friends. He made a tour through the country near Chambersburg, collecting money, and often engaging in religious controversy with those who met him and presumed to attack his creed. He was now a much better debater than formerly; and as he had learned some theology, he met and defeated, to the great delight of his co-religionists, many a village declaimer against "Popery." The funds were so generously contributed that Father Dubois was soon able to rebuild the college; and in 1826 a new structure arose on the ruins of the old one.

As a seminarian, Mr. Hughes not only cultivated controversy, but also the muse of poetry, and we have several of his productions published at this time in "The Adams Centinel," at Gettysburg. We shall give specimens of them in a future chapter.

CHAPTER III.

HE IS ORDAINED A PRIEST, BECOMES RECTOR OF A PARISH, AND ENCOUNTERS THE TRUSTEE SYSTEM IN PHILADELPHIA.

MR. HUGHES was ordained a deacon in 1825, by the Bishop of Philadelphia, Right-Rev. Doctor Conwell, who immediately took him with him in a visitation of the diocese. They travelled through Pennsylvania chiefly on horseback, for in those days there were neither railways nor stages in many parts of the country. The sturdy deacon rather enjoyed the tour among the great valleys and the wild mountains. The bishop insisted that he should preach wherever they went. The deacon had therefore to preach his first sermon on the missions in a log-church at a place called Path Valley, where the bishop gave the sacrament of confirmation to a number of children and adults. It was the only sermon he had ready; and as there was little time to prepare another in their travels, he preached it everywhere, to the amusement of the pleasant bishop, who jocosely called it the "Cuckoo Sermon,"—for the cuckoo has only a note or two in the compass of its voice.

At Chambersburg, he found a tract called "Protestantism and Popery," and he at once undertook to refute its charges against the Church. He published his answer to the tract in the "United States Catholic Miscellany," of Charleston, and afterward republished it as a pamphlet with the title "An Answer to Nine Objections made by an Anonymous Writer against the Catholic Religion, by a clergyman of Chambersburg, Franklin Co." This pamphlet was printed in Philadelphia a few months after Mr. Hughes's ordination to the priesthood. This event took place on Oct. 15, 1826, in St. Joseph's Church, Philadelphia. Right-Rev. Henry Conwell, the bishop of the see, was the ordaining prelate. At last the goal of John Hughes's early aspirations was reached. The persevering Irish peasant was now Father Hughes, and the field was open for the display of all his talents and religious zeal. He was appointed first an assistant to Rev. Dr. Hurley, pastor of St. Augustine's Church, Philadelphia, who soon learned to appreciate his abilities and worth. About the same time one of his professors at Mount St. Mary's, Father Dubois, was made Bishop of New York.

From St. Augustine's, where he had distinguished himself by perseverance in labour, by love of books, by zeal, and by skill in controversy, Father Hughes was transferred to Bedford, to take the place of the Rev. Father Heyden, promoted to a city parish in Philadelphia. In the mountainous regions of his new mission the young priest toiled unceasingly. He met everywhere, Lutheran and Calvinistic settlers imbued with bitter prejudices against his religion. Everywhere he defended it by tongue and pen, and his courage and manliness won their admiration, and the love of his poor flock. In 1827 he was recalled to Philadelphia, where a storm of ecclesiastical disputes was raging. The experience which he gained on this occasion taught him prudence, and how to act afterward in the battles which he fought in New York.

The Catholic Churches in Philadelphia were then managed by what is known in the history of the Church in the United States as the "trustee system." This system deprived the bishop and the clergy of the control of ecclesiastical affairs, and gave it to laymen chosen by the pewholders. Consequently the pewholders were often divided into factions, and the election for trustees frequently turned the Churches into political meeting houses. Unprincipled men took advantage of this state of affairs, and sometimes Catholics only in name controlled the Church property, paid the priests' salaries, and claimed to control clerical appointments to office, in spite of the pastor appointed by the bishop, and in spite of the bishop himself. Nearly all the Catholic congregations of the time were torn by scandals and controversies, owing to this system. When Bishop Conwell, in 1820, went to Philadelphia, he found his Cathedral of St. Mary's in charge of a popular but unworthy priest named Hogan. The bishop suspended him; but the trustees and a part of the people refused to recognize the episcopal suspension. According to the civil law, the board of trustees should consist of eight laymen, annually elected by the pewholders, and of not more than three priests, the mode of whose election was not specified. The bishop claimed the right to appoint or remove these three, according to the custom of the Church; but the lay-trustees claimed the right for themselves. Hogan urged them to take possession of the Cathedral. This they did; and the bishop with his faithful clergy retired to the neighbouring Church of St. Joseph.

Even after Hogan had publicly left the Church, married a wife, and become a Protestant, in 1824, the disorders continued. Unfortunately for Philadelphia, Bishop Conwell was a man of weak character. Worn out by the length of the conflict with the trustees, he made an illegal and uncanonical surrender of his rights. The trustees rejoiced; but the faithful clergy and laity mourned. It was at this time that Father Hughes was brought back from the mountains to the city, and made pastor, first, of St. Joseph's Church, and soon after, of St. Mary's, still disturbed by the turbulent trustees. Father Heyden, disgusted with them, had left and gone back to his old parish, rural and peaceful Bedford. The new pastor of St. Mary's, after a short experience with the rebels, also judged it wiser to leave them severely alone. He therefore retired, and the bishop would give them no priest. Consequently the congregation deserted St. Mary's. Rome, to which appeals had been made, soon acted, and condemned the weak and uncanonical concessions made by the bishop, and "determined," in the words of Father Hughes, "that the bishop should be bishop in spite of himself."

In a letter to Father Bruté, written at this time, the future archbishop thus expressed his feelings: —

"What will become of the Church if laymen, sometimes as depraved as they are ignorant, have such influence in her government? What will become of the clergy, if they must descend from their sacred character, and become parties and the tools of parties in the petty broils of contending rivals for the office of trustee? And for what advantage? Just to have the choosing of their masters. There is no remedy for all this until the time shall have come to aim the blow, not at the branches, but at the root of this abominable system of trusteeing Churches."

At this time an incident occured worthy of special note. Bishop Conwell was summoned to Rome, and

THE TRUSTEE SYSTEM. 37

an administrator appointed in his place. Harold and Ryan, two insubordinate Dominican priests who had been officiating in St. Mary's Church, were removed from Philadelphia by order of their superior, the vicar-general of their order, and of the Pope, and sent to Cincinnati. The two suspended priests appealed to the United States government against the papal order. Mr. Adams, who was then our president, instructed the American minister at Paris to bring the appeal before the papal nuncio there; but as the nuncio clearly showed that the case was of a purely spiritual character, of pure ecclesiastical jurisdiction, and not within the domain of the civil power, Mr. Henry Clay, then Secretary of State, ordered the minister at Paris to have nothing more to do with the affair.

Bishop Conwell remained at Rome nearly a year, then returned to Philadelphia, where he died in 1842, at the venerable age of ninety-four. The Pope never restored jurisdiction to the weak but well-meaning old bishop. Priests Harold and Ryan soon after submitted to their superiors, and the case against them was closed. But the effects of their scandal long continued.

During all these troubles Father Hughes worked zealously in his parish, and fought for his Church. He strove to remove the prejudices against her, which he knew existed in the minds of even well-meaning Americans. He strove to put her doctrines before the American mind in their true colours. For this purpose, in addition to his parochial duties, he tried to found a tract society for the publication of cheap Catholic literature of a controversial character. He wrote for this purpose a religious tale, to counteract the supposed influence of a small Protestant novel published in England, republished in this country, and circulated freely among the poor Catholics. The hero was Andrew Dunn, who, it was feigned, had become a Protestant because the priest had horse-whipped him for doubting certain articles of the Catholic Creed. After the whipping, Andrew takes to reading the Bible, frequents the society of the godly, soon sees the errors of "Popery," and becomes a match for all the Roman theologians. Father Hughes knew that, although this novel was stupid, it would do harm, and that all its calumnies would be believed by prejudiced minds. He therefore made merely a slight change in the title of the story and called it, "The Conversion and Edifying Death of Andrew Dunn." The plot of this work and of the original is poorly constructed. But the future archbishop shows in his production that familiarity with the weapons of theological war, and that vigour of reasoning, which always distinguished him. Andrew, in going through the process of reconversion, and in preparing himself for an edifying death in the bosom of the Mother Church, asks his Protestant friends to solve his doubts and to answer his questions. How does he know that his understanding of the Bible is the right one? How can a Church that is only three hundred years old be the true one? And how can any one say in the Creed, "I believe in the Holy Catholic Church," if he is not a member of it? Andrew prays for light, realizes that the Bible is not its own interpreter, and that the only interpreter is the Infallible Church, that the book cannot interpret itself, that it needs a reliable interpreter as the law requires a competent judge to decide its meaning. He concludes, therefore, with Melanchthon and Henry IV. of France, that the " Infallible Church is the only reliable interpreter of the Bible, and the safest one to die in."

Father Hughes, like most young authors, was enthusiastic over his first book. He imagined that it was going to have a wide circulation, and convert the whole country to the Catholic Church. He wrote at once to his old professor, Father Bruté, sending him five dollars' worth of copies of "Andrew Dunn." But Father Bruté could neither sell the copies, nor pay for them, and Father Hughes, finding his first tract a failure, discontinued his efforts to found a Catholic publication society. He made more converts in Philadelphia by his tongue than by his pen. In his letters written at this time he speaks of many men and women who joined the Church after hearing him explain Catholic doctrines from the pulpit.

While busy with his pen, he was also indefatigable in works of charity. In 1829 he founded St. John's Orphan Asylum, and five years afterward he writes of it in the "Catholic Herald":—

" This asylum, since the period of its establishment, has afforded home, protection, food, clothing, and education to a number of destitute orphans, varying from twenty to twenty-eight. It has, besides this, afforded the benefits of religious instruction and gratuitous education to more than one thousand female children. The money to support it has been derived from the subscriptions of the original society, from private donations, from the sale of fancy articles manufactured by the Sisters themselves, and from the proceeds of five charity sermons, together with one or two inconsiderable legacies of a hundred dollars each."

A hard-working pastor of souls was Father Hughes. His time was occupied from morning to night listening to the tales of woe which misery poured into his ear, settling disputes in families, comforting the sick and the dying day and night.

No pastor was ever more punctual or faithful than he in attending to all the varied duties of a Catholic priest in a large city parish. He was indeed equal to the task, which was but a preliminary to greater and more conspicuous duties in the higher office which he soon attained. Everything that concerned the welfare of his fellowman, but especially what concerned his adopted country, interested him. He also particularly remembered Ireland, the land of his birth. Her sorrows affected him deeply, and he always rejoiced in whatever improved the condition of her long-oppressed people.

CHAPTER IV.

HIS INTEREST IN IRISH CATHOLIC EMANCIPATION. — CONTROVERSY WITH DOCTOR DELANCEY. — HIS LETTERS TO "THE PROTESTANT."

FATHER HUGHES, who had suffered, and who had seen his countrymen suffer, under the English penal laws, was filled with joy when he heard of the passage of the Catholic Emancipation Bill, through the English parliament. George IV. signed the bill on April 13, 1829, and as soon as the news reached America a solemn Mass of thanksgiving was celebrated in St. Augustine's Church, Philadelphia, on the 31st of May. Father Hughes preached the sermon from the text: "Lord, thou hast blessed the land, thou hast turned away the captivity of Jacob. . . . Mercy and truth have met each other: justice and peace have kissed. Truth is sprung out of the earth; and justice hath looked down from Heaven."[1] This, his first printed sermon, was dedicated to Daniel O'Connell. It made Father Hughes's reputation as an orator, and was the occasion of one of his controversies. The

[1] Psalm lxxxiv.

"Church Register," organ of the Philadelphia Episcopalians, and then edited by Rev. W. H. Delancey, D. D., attacked the Catholics on the occasion of their emancipation, and in a series of articles expressed fears and regrets in consequence of their restoration to citizenship in the British Empire. Father Hughes replied with vigour in a series of letters to the " United States Gazette," and thenceforward seemed to consider it his duty to reply to every attack on his religion.

In October, 1829, the first provincial council of American bishops was held in Baltimore; and Father Hughes was present, as one of the theologians to Very Rev. Father Matthews, the administrator of the diocese of Philadelphia. The old Bishop Conwell, while in Rome, had recommended Father Hughes for his successor; but the Pope appointed the Rev. Francis Patrick Kenrick, president of a theological seminary at Bardstown, Kentucky, as coadjutor to Bishop Conwell and administrator of the diocese. Father Kenrick, then in his thirty-second year, six months younger than Father Hughes, was consecrated as titular Bishop of Arath, *in partibus infidelium*, at Bardstown, by Bishop Flaget on June 6, 1830. Bishop Kenrick afterward became Archbishop of Baltimore. He has the reputation of having been the best theologian in the American Church. He wrote, among other works, text-books of theology and a translation of the Bible. A man of great modesty, he shunned controversy and publicity. The schismatics of Philadelphia soon yielded to his gentle but forcible sway.

About this time Father Hughes wrote a letter to his sister Ellen, who had become a Sister of Charity under the name of Sister Mary Angela. He tells her of his work in the city of brotherly love, and of the numerous converts whom he was receiving into the Church, and adds the very truthful and striking statement that, "If the Catholics themselves were what they should be, the number of converts would be astonishing." He was soon engaged in another controversy. This time his opponent was one of his own creed and profession, a prominent Catholic priest of New York, the Rev. Thomas C. Levins. The occasion of this controversy was peculiar, and Father Hughes was often blamed for his part in it. The following are the facts.

There was published in New York at that time a newspaper approved by many of the ministers of the city, and called "The Protestant." It made weekly attacks on the Catholic Church, and published all kinds of scandalous stories about priests and nuns, without taking the trouble to find out whether they were true or not. Many respectable Protestants denounced it for its scurrility and mendacity. Father Hughes, in a spirit of genuine Irish mischief, determined to humbug "The Protestant" and expose it by sending from Philadelphia, under the pseudonym of "Crammer," a number of absurd communications on the growth of "Popery," giving coloured reports of Catholic ceremonies and institutions. The Philadelphia correspondent wrote like an over-zealous Protestant. In one letter "Crammer" told how the four "Mass-houses" there were made to hold twelve congregations, "and that there was an extra Mass late in the afternoon." He described an imaginary nunnery in Cambria County, Pa., and a Jesuit college in Pittsburgh, where none existed. "The Protestant," as is usual with newspapers of that class, swallowed the bait, and on March 13, praised the truthfulness and zeal of its most reliable correspondent. It said: —

"Our Philadelphia friend communicates his melancholy intelligence in a very evangelical spirit of sensibility and fervour. We trust 'Crammer' will remember that his letters are sermons of momentous importance, and that they are now read with intense and increasing interest by a rapidly increasing host of Protestants of a like spirit. The oftener we decorate our columns with such pathetic appeals and heart-stirring facts, the more encouragement we shall feel to blow the trumpet in Zion and sound the alarm in the Holy Mountain. We hope our correspondent will supply us with plenty of ammunition, and it shall be discharged to produce the desired effect."

Again the enthusiastic editor writes: "We have received a number of inquiries for our friend 'Crammer,' and in reply we are highly gratified to exhibit this genuine Protestant of the city of Penn *in propria persona*," and then follows a communication from "Crammer" himself, containing the usual fables.

After deceiving the credulous journalist for some time, Father Hughes came out in his own name and excused himself for imposing on the credulity of "The Protestant," by stating that he wished to show how ready the newspaper and its supporters were to believe any story, no matter how absurd, against the Catholic Church. Many Catholics, — and particularly Father Levins, — however, blamed him for what they considered an undignified act; and he himself regretted what he had done, although it had the effect of making the slanderous newspaper ridiculous.

Bishop Kenrick in the first visitation of his diocese was accompanied by Father Hughes, who had the pleasure of preaching before his venerable father and mother in the church at Chambersburg. The bishop and the priest visited Bedford, Pittsburgh, and Blairsville, and stopped for a time with Father Galitzin, a Russian prince and convert who had founded a Catholic settlement at Lorretto, in the Alleghany Mountains. After this visitation, Father Hughes acted for a time as secretary to the bishop, and agent for Mount St. Mary's College. He was always occupied. At this time he began a series of sermons on the evidences of Christianity; and Jews as well as Protestants flocked to hear him.

The "trustees" still made trouble in Philadelphia, especially in St. Mary's Church, so that the bishop was obliged to put it under an interdict, and order "the cessation from all sacred functions in the church and cemeteries of St. Mary's." Father Hughes stood at the right hand of the bishop in this conflict, and the trustees had to yield. At first they gave up their claim to the right of appointing the pastors; and then Father Hughes built a new church without lay-trustees, and thus completely conquered the rebels. He began the work in 1821; and in May of that year the bishop laid the corner-stone and named the church St. John's. It became the fashionable church of the city, and St. Mary's, with its turbulent trustees, was almost deserted. St. John's was dedicated in 1832. The Rev. Dr. Power of St. Peter's, New York, preached the dedication sermon. The new parish was heavily in debt; but a Mr. Frenaye, a West Indian of French origin, gave his whole fortune to help Father Hughes. Another friend gave him what was then considered a very large subscription amounting to five thousand dollars.

The zealous pastor, surrounded by friends and admirers, amid all his cares and duties did not forget his own spiritual and mental improvement. He gives us a knowledge of his private habits in a letter to his old friend Father Bruté written on July 28, 1832: "Parties of pleasure . . . are not frequented by me, and except one, I am sure I visit less than any clergyman in this city." If he had a leisure hour after reading his breviary, he devoted it to the study of theology, especially to that part of it which deals with the questions in dispute between Catholics and Protestants. Thus he prepared himself for the arena of conflict. He knew the Catholic arguments well, and so well-equipped himself that he was a match for the distinguished Presbyterian clergyman, Rev. Dr. Breckenridge, who soon became his first great opponent in the field of controversy.

CHAPTER V.

THE BRECKENRIDGE CONTROVERSY. — FATHER HUGHES PROPOSED FOR BISHOP OF CINCINNATI.

IN the controversy with Dr. Breckenridge, this learned divine had many advantages. He belonged to a very aristocratic and talented family; he had received a fine classical education in the best schools. He was a very prominent clergyman in his own sect; and conscious of great talent and great eloquence, he and his friends rather despised the plebeian Irishman whose friends were very poor and who was a minister of the hated Church of Rome. In those days "No Popery:" was a very popular cry.

The origin of the controversy was as follows: An anti-Catholic tale, called "Father Clement," was published by a Protestant book-concern, and then severely reviewed by a Catholic layman. Dr. Breckenridge reviewed the reviewer in the "Christian Advocate," and made the following challenge in his article: "There are priests and bishops. We are willing to meet any one of them on the broad field of this vital discussion." A friend of Father Hughes who had read the challenge, presumed, without consulting him, to tell others that Father Hughes would reply to the Presbyterian Champion. The subject to be discussed was, "The Rule of Religious Faith."

All of Father Hughes's old friends — some from fear of his lack of ability, others from natural aversion to controversies — tried to dissuade him from the discussion. But he felt chivalrously bound to stand by the promise of his friend, and he would not recede even though he had no organ in which to publish his answers to the doctor's attacks.

Some friends in this emergency founded the "Catholic Herald," and thus the Catholics of Philadelphia were enabled to read the arguments of their champion. His first letter to the doctor contained a characteristic postscript : " You take great pains," he writes, " to show, in all your letters, how much you have to do, and how much leisure — ' sanctuary quietude ' — remains on my hands, intimating thereby the advantage which my situation gives me over you in the conducting of this controversy. Be assured, Reverend Sir, that if I thought the public could be interested in the details of my avocations, I also could make out a tolerable list of duties, enough perhaps to turn the scales of comparison. But to make your mind easy on the subject of your official occupations, I beg to state that I am prepared to sustain the Catholic argument, if God gives me health, against any or all the clergymen of the synod or general assembly, provided he or they write with your signature and adhere to the rules." The controversy ceased in September, by the retreat of Dr. Breckenridge from the field; and Father Hughes was generally admitted to have gained a victory. It made him famous. The Catholics, especially in Philadelphia and throughout the country, recognized in him a leader able to defend them from the attacks of all their enemies. His name was soon after sent to Rome, as one of the candidates for the vacant see of Cincinnati. But Rome's choice was his friend Dr. Purcell, who was consecrated bishop in 1833.

Dr. Breckenridge was not satisfied with the result of the written controversy. He felt the opprobrium of reputed defeat, and longed for a second opportunity to retrieve his injured reputation as a controversialist by conquering the famous priest. Father Hughes soon gave the desired opportunity. He was invited to deliver a lecture, and chose as the subject of it: "Whether the Roman Catholic Religion is favourable to Civil and Religious Liberty?" Dr. Breckenridge saw the announcement, and at once wrote the following challenge : —

NEW YORK, January 21, 1835.

SIR, — I have just been informed that you are expected to address a society, to-morrow evening, on a question of which the following is the substance, — "Whether the Roman Catholic Religion is favourable to Civil and Religious Liberty?"

I write a few lines in order to say that I will meet you on the evening of the 29th instant, before the same society, Providence permitting, on that question, — or if that be not *agreeable* to you, in any other place where this vital question may be fully discussed before our fellow-citizens.

As I shall not be present, I request that you will yourself make the necessary suggestions to the society, to-morrow evening, and give me as early a reply as convenient. I can conceive of only one reason for your refusing, and I hope time has overcome that.

I remain, your obedient servant,

JOHN BRECKENRIDGE.

Father Hughes did not wish to accept this challenge. Some of his best friends disapproved altogether of these disputes, which often only excited passion and did more harm than good. Besides, was he equipped for an oral debate with one of the most eloquent Presbyterian divines of the day? Some doubted it. He felt himself that his theological education was not perfect. Still he came of fighting stock, and he was not a man to be cowed by any opponent. Besides he was conscious of native logical power, which is often more efficacious than mere erudition in questions of this kind. He therefore accepted the challenge; and the dispute lasted six nights. Once engaged in it, Father Hughes threw away fear, and argued with great force against the proud divine, who tried to browbeat and bully him from the very beginning.

"Allow me," said Dr. Breckenridge, "thus early in the debate, to say that nothing but the love of liberty as an American, and of truth as a Protestant Christian, could induce me to subject my feelings to the coarse and ill-bred impertinence of a priesthood whose temper and treatment toward other men alternate between servility to their sovereigns and oppression of their unhappy subjects.

"I can and will bear, for the sake of the great cause, whatever may be made necessary — though, thank God, I am not forced to do it either as a minion of the Pope, or the subject of a narrow and vulgar Jesuitism." This insult roused the fighting blood of John Hughes. It was dangerous for any antagonist to abuse him, or try to be sarcastic at his expense. He was a master of irony, and could be bitterly sarcastic. "Do you not, sir, pity the gentleman," — he replied, in a strong and cutting tone, his sturdy form erect, his eye flashing, and his finger pointing at his opponent, — "the Chesterfield of the Presbyterian Church, the *magister elegantiarum*, about to be exposed to the retorts of a Catholic priest?"

His tone, his manner, his defiant look, drove Dr. Breckenridge frantic. He so far forgot himself as to call Father Hughes "a blackguard, coarse and impertinent."

Father Hughes replied with consummate sarcasm and great eloquence. A learned Jesuit named

Kenney helped him in gathering the facts and arguments in this controversy; but Bishop Kenrick, naturally of a peaceful disposition, never liked it, and tried to stop it.

In spite of the hard blows he gave to the Protestant creeds, Father Hughes was very popular with the Protestants of Philadelphia, who admired him for his ability and courtesy; and particularly as they were Americans, they admired him for his fearlessness and pluck. His company was much sought after by the prominent people of the city; and invitations to dinner were numerous on his desk. He was such a good talker, so affable and so witty, that all admired him. He would sing a good song, too, if the company was select; but at the same time he was always a zealous pastor of souls, and a faithful administrator of a parish.

The debts of his parish weighed heavily on him. His people were poor; he saw no way out of his financial troubles except by seeking aid away from home. He then thought of Mexico, where Catholics were rich; and he determined to go there and seek help for his debt-burdened people. In order to fit himself for this task, he applied himself to the study of Spanish. But when his loving flock heard of his purpose to leave them, they redoubled their exertions, paid off all the pressing debts, and kept him at home.

CHAPTER VI.

HE IS MADE COADJUTOR TO THE BISHOP OF NEW YORK.

THE Catholic population in the United States had grown so rapidly that it became necessary to increase the number of dioceses. It was proposed to make Pittsburgh an episcopal see, and Father Hughes was named for it. He was at the same time named as one of the three candidates for the coadjutorship to the old bishop of New York, Dr. Dubois. The other two candidates were Father Mulledy, a learned Jesuit, and Bishop Kenrick, the coadjutor of Dr. Conwell of Philadelphia. The choice of Dr. Dubois was either Father Mulledy or Bishop Kenrick, who wished to get away from Philadelphia, where his relations with the feeble-minded old bishop were no longer pleasant. Dr. Kenrick had even asked Rome for a division of the Philadelphia diocese, his own transfer to the new see of Pittsburgh, and the appointment in his place of Father Hughes as coadjutor to Bishop Conwell. But although Bishop Kenrick's request was granted by the Sacred Congregation of the Propaganda, the

Pope, on account of objections made by Bishop England, of Charleston, refused to sanction the transfer, and the whole plan miscarried. Dr. Kenrick at the same time wrote to Rome, withdrawing Father Hughes's name from the list of the candidates for the See of Pittsburgh. This gave rise to a report that Bishop Kenrick was opposed to Father Hughes's promotion. Statements to this effect found their way into the newspapers, which blamed Bishop Kenrick for Father Hughes's failure to be made Bishop of Pittsburgh. He at once took notice of the rumours, and wrote to Dr. Kenrick a letter in which he says: —

"You could not suppose that it would have pained me not to be made Bishop of Pittsburgh, since you remember that last Spring I wished you to write such a letter in my name and at my request. I had studied the inside as well as the outside of a mitre, and I regarded him who is obliged to wear it, as entitled to pity, not envy. I had, if not humility, at least sense enough to be satisfied that the man who is qualified and willing to be a bishop in the United States, deserves a recompense which he may not expect from this ungrateful world."

Shortly after the date of this letter, the Council of Baltimore, on the 16th of April, 1837, sent his name with two others to Rome for the coadjutorship of New York, and on November 31, following, he received notice of his selection by the Pope, for that arduous office. A few weeks after he told the news to his flock, who were all in tears at the thought of being separated from him. They had become devotedly attached to him. His popularity was great in the whole city. Many of the most prominent people invited him to their houses, and vied for the honour of having him spend his last evenings in Philadelphia with them. But true to his nature, which was sincere, and faithful to early friendship, he spent his last nights in Philadelphia in the house of a poor man whose acquaintance he had made while a day-labourer at Emmittsburg.

He was consecrated at New York, Jan. 7, 1838, in St. Patrick's Church, then the Cathedral in Mott Street. Bishop Dubois was the consecrating bishop, assisted by Bishops Kenrick, of Philadelphia, and Fenwick, of Boston. The sermon was preached by the distinguished Jesuit Father Mulledy, of Georgetown College. The new prelate received the title of Bishop of Basileopolis and Coadjutor to the Bishop of New York. Archbishop McCloskey, in the funeral sermon over Bishop Hughes, thus eloquently describes him on the day of his consecration : —

"I remember how all eyes were fixed, how all eyes were strained, to get a glimpse of their newly consecrated bishop; and as they saw that dignified and manly countenance; as they beheld those features beaming with the light of intellect, bearing already upon them the impress of that force of character which peculiarly marked him throughout his life, that firmness of resolution, that unalterable and unbending will, and yet blending at the same time that great benignity and suavity of expression; when they marked the quiet composure and self-possession of every look and every gesture, of his whole gait and demeanor, — all hearts were drawn and warmed toward him. Every pulse within that vast assembly, both of clergy and of laity, was quickened with a higher sense of courage and of hope. Every breast was filled with joy, and as it were with a new and younger might."

The diocese of New York at that time comprised the whole State of New York and about half of New Jersey. The Catholic population in this territory was about two hundred thousand. There were forty priests and about twenty churches. Fifteen of these priests and eight of the churches were on the Island of Manhattan. New York and Albany had a few parochial schools, under the charge of the Sisters of Charity. New York, Brooklyn, Albany, and Utica had Catholic orphan asylums; elsewhere in the diocese there was no Catholic institution of education or of charity. To-day there are eight bishops, nearly three hundred churches, about five hundred priests, and a Catholic population of nearly two millions in the territory once comprised in the diocese of New York. A college founded by Bishop Dubois, at Nyack on the Hudson, in 1833, was destroyed by fire and never rebuilt, as it had not been successful.

The "trustee system" flourished in all its viciousness; the churches were deeply in debt, and the lay-trustees and the bishop were often in open warfare. A schismatical spirit had spread among the Catholics, who were disunited and discouraged. They were chiefly of the poorer class of emigrants from Ireland, and the degradation of the penal laws was still evident in their condition. The old bishop had few natural ties of sympathy with them. He was a Frenchman, and did not understand the people well enough to govern them. He had become paralyzed, and was not able, although he was originally a man of force and courage, to sustain the conflict with "trusteeism" and insubordinate priests. Gradually the whole administration of the diocese fell on the broad shoulders of the sturdy coadjutor, who never feared a foe or shunned a fight when the interests of his Church, of his native land, or of his adopted country, were in question.

Having felt the want of education in his early days, his first effort was to establish a theological seminary. He afterward modified his plan so as to make it a secular as well as a theological college. It was opened Sept. 20, 1838, at Lafargeville in Jefferson County, under the name of "St. Vincent de Paul's Seminary," and placed under the charge of three priests, Fathers Guth, Moran (afterward Vicar-General of Newark), and Haes, and of three tutors. But

Lafargeville was too far away from the centres of population to be suitable for a school; so after a short experiment the seminary was closed.

The next thing that engaged his attention was the quarrel between Bishop Dubois and the trustees of his cathedral. One of the priests attached to it, Rev. Mr. Levins, the same who had criticised Father Hughes's letters to "The Protestant" was suspended for insubordination; but the trustees refused to recognize the validity of the episcopal act, or to admit any priest to officiate in Father Levins's place. They made him rector of the parochial school, paid him a salary, refused to pay his successor appointed by the bishop, and threatened to cut off even the bishop's salary, if he would not yield to their demands. Under their instructions, Levins expelled from the Sunday-school a teacher appointed by the bishop. The civil law authorized the trustees to do this; it authorized them even to bring in a constable and expel a priest from the sanctuary if they thought it necessary. Bishop Dubois, usually very tenacious of his own rights, and unwilling to give any of his authority to his coadjutor, was very glad to let him fight this battle alone. The young coadjutor attacked the trustees and appealed to the congregation against them. He called a meeting of the pewholders and thus addressed them: —

"Is it your intention that such power be exercised by your trustees? If so it is almost time for the ministers of God to forsake your temple and erect an altar to their God around which religion shall be free, the Council of Trent fully recognized, and the laws of the Church applied to the government and regulation of the Church."

It was a question whether the legislature of the State or the bishop should govern the Church. The trustees persisted in their uncanonical proceedings. On Feb. 10, 1839, they called in a constable to turn out the bishop's Catechist from the cathedral Sunday-school. On the Sunday following, Bishop Hughes noted the fact from the pulpit, and demanded an apology from the trustees; but they made none. On Sunday, February 24, of the same year, he read from the altar a pastoral letter signed by Bishop Dubois, but written by himself, in which he called on the people to condemn the act of their so-called representatives, and threatened the rebels with excommunication. He then called a meeting of the pewholders. It was largely attended, and the bishop made a long speech in which he proved the right of the Church authorities to appoint or remove all those who were to exercise spiritual functions. He showed that the trustees had violated the laws and the discipline of the Church in removing the bishop's Catechist. He pointed out the danger of permitting State interference with Church affairs, and roused his audience by an allusion which won for him at once their hearts and their approval. He spoke of the Irish penal laws, and described the Church of England as "a gilded slave chained to the throne," while Irish Catholics, rather than sacrifice the freedom of their religion, worshipped in mountain solitudes, or in secluded valleys, around the priest upon whose head the State had set the same price as on the head of a wolf. Would they be false to the traditions of their loyal and self-sacrificing forefathers; or would they allow the State constable to appoint their priests and their teachers? A ringing cheer and shouts of "noes" was the answer. A resolution condemning the action of the trustees was carried without objection; and the new election which soon followed placed in power a board of trustees obedient to the bishop and in perfect harmony with his will. This victory broke the power of the trustees in New York; for although from time to time in some churches they gave trouble, they were never after able to oppose his authority or resist his orders with success. On March 20, 1839, he had so completely defeated the rebels that he wrote to his friend Mr. Frenaye, in Philadelphia: "We have brought the trustees so low that they are not able to give even a decent kick."

Bishop Dubois soon became unfit for duty. He was paralyzed, and his mind was no longer sound. In consequence of this condition of affairs, the Pope took away from him all jurisdiction, and transferred it to Bishop Hughes. In August, 1839, Archbishop Eccleston, of Baltimore, visited New York, bringing the Pope's orders. The venerable and saintly bishop obeyed them, although it was a great humiliation for him who might be called "the Father of the American Clergy," to have to give up his power to one whom he had known twenty years before as a poor Irish emigrant.

Bishop Hughes was visiting the Northern part of the State when he heard the news that he had been appointed, by the Holy See, Administrator of New York. In this visitation he found many interesting facts which he often related to his friends. For instance, in Onondaga County he found a Catholic colony composed of eighteen converts from Protestantism. There was no priest nearer to them than sixty miles; and they owed their conversion to a Catholic pedler who, in the year 1836, spent a night in the house of the head of the colony. The bishop wrote an account of this colony for the "Annals of the Propagation of the Faith," in the year 1840.

On October 14, of the same year, he published a pastoral letter in which he spoke of the resignation of Bishop Dubois in the following sympathetic terms:

"Having passed through more than half a century of apostolical labour and boundless as well as untiring zeal, he was entitled at the age of seventy-six years, and it was natural for him to seek, the privilege of repose, by leaving to younger energies to take up the burden which he had so long and so zealously sustained."

CHAPTER VII.

HE GOES TO EUROPE. — HIS INTERVIEW WITH O'CONNELL. — HIS GREAT CONTROVERSY ON THE SCHOOL QUESTION.

THE zeal of the bishop increased with his responsibilities. His people were poor, and his diocese heavily in debt. He therefore determined to cross the Atlantic, and seek help from the wealthy Catholics of Europe. Consequently he sailed for Havre, on the 16th of October, 1839, in the packet ship "Louis Philippe." It was on this voyage that he wrote at sea the description of a storm. The reader will find the description in the thirteenth chapter.

On his arrival in Europe, he spent some time in Paris, and was presented to the king and to the royal family by our ambassador, Gen. Lewis Cass. In January, 1840, the bishop was in Rome, where he remained nearly three months. The Pope treated him with great consideration, and gave him many presents. In April of the same year he went to

Vienna, in Austria, to seek aid from the "Leopoldine Society," — so named after Leopoldina, Archduchess of Austria, and Empress of Brazil. This society was organized in 1829, for the promotion of Catholic missions in America. To this society he made an address in which he spoke of the wants of his diocese. He said: "There should be one church, at least, and one pastor for every two thousand souls." He received a large donation for his new college and seminary of St. John's, at Fordham, and was welcomed with honour in the Austrian capital. Here he made the acquaintance of Monsignore Bedini, who afterward came to this country as papal nuncio. He met also Marshal Nugent, a distinguished Irish soldier in the service of Austria, and the great statesman, Metternich.

In May the bishop returned to Paris. Later he went to London, where he met the Irish Liberator, Daniel O'Connell. Both of them soon afterward made speeches from the same platform at a meeting of the Catholic Institute of Great Britain, in London. The bishop in this address gave a brief sketch of the progress of the Church in America. In a few days he left England for Ireland. On June 1, 1840, he writes from Dublin: —

"I am in the capital of poor old Ireland; and they tell me wonderful things of the moral revolution which has taken place on the subject of temperance. It is remarkable that this nation which has been thought the most in need of this reformation, has embraced it with a unanimity and cordiality resembling that with which they received the Christian faith. Already, I am told, the number is one million and a half of those who, lest they should violate the divine command prohibiting excess, have embraced the counsel to abstain altogether. And the astonishing fact has been mentioned to me by high authority; namely, that the Scotch, who are considered a sober people, have been in times past in the habit of consuming, man for man, nearly double the quantity of spirituous liquors that was consumed by the Irish. This has been established repeatedly by parliamentary documents and evidence."

The bishop returned to his diocese on July 18, and found his flock engaged in a zealous effort to change the school system from which they were suffering in the city and in the State. The Catholics thought and felt that there is a radical defect in any system of education which omits religion. It is Catholic belief that morality should be taught in the school, and that morality cannot be separated from religious doctrine. Hence, Catholics always insist on having their children instructed in the creed of their parents; and no system of education will ever satisfy them which does not fulfil this condition. They hold that morality depends on dogmatic teaching; morality implies law, and law implies God, the legislator who is behind all sanction to law. The ten commandments are moral laws, every one of which rests on a dogmatic truth, on the existence of God, on the immortality of the soul, and on the inspired character of the Sacred Scriptures from which the Mosaic and the Christian precepts are taken. For Catholics, therefore, no secular education, no matter how perfect, will be satisfactory unless accompanied with religious instruction. They are as much opposed to divorce between science and religion in the school, as to divorce between husband and wife in the family. Nor have Catholics ever been able to understand why orthodox Hebrews or orthodox Protestants should not agree with them in demanding that the education of children shall be religious as well as secular. It was universally so in the Colonial times, and in the early days of our Republic. The schools in all the thirteen original Colonies were religious and denominational. Hence, as a historical fact, the true American system of public education was denominational and sectarian; and the attempt to substitute for it a godless, infidel, or agnostic system, is foreign to our republic, and contrary to all the best traditions of the country.

When Bishop Hughes entered into the controversy on the school question, the Public School Society of New York professed to teach religion without sectarianism. This he considered a most illogical proceeding. He wrote to the gentlemen who formed the society:

"If you exclude all sects, you exclude Christianity. Take away the distinctive dogmas of the Catholics, the Baptists, the Methodists, the Presbyterians and so on, and you have nothing left but deism." Even the reading of the Bible in the schools is an act of sectarianism. There is a dispute among the sects as to which version is correct. On this question, Catholics and Protestants are radically divided. If you read the New Testament, you insult the Hebrew children, and if you leave it out of the Bible you ignore the Christians. No matter how homœopathically small the dose of religion you give the children, it will be always sectarian.

But while the public schools of those days professed to be non-sectarian, they were really Protestant institutions, used to pervert Catholics. The Protestant version of the Bible used in them was King James's, which Catholics hold to be incomplete and false. It was read every morning in the presence of the Catholic children; and the teachers, who were all Protestants, made comments on the text unfriendly and insulting to Catholic convictions. Protestant hymns were sung, and Protestant prayers, expressing Protestant doctrines, were recited. The whole tendency of this system of education was to make Catholic children indifferent to their religion or apostates from it.

The Catholic clergy and laity therefore opposed these schools, and began to establish the present parochial system of education. In spite of their poverty they built parochial schools. If they were unable to build, they opened schools in the basements of their churches. In 1840 the number of children attending these schools was about five thousand, out of the ten thousand children of school-age. Many of these attended the public schools with great peril to their faith; others did not go to school at all.

Before the bishop's return from Europe, a priest of Albany wrote to the Vicar-General of New York, Dr. Power, Rector of St. Peter's Church in Barclay Street, telling him that he thought the Catholics could get some of the general school fund by petitioning the legislature. Some of the members of it had expressed views friendly to Catholic claims for a share of the money raised by taxation for school purposes, and considered it unjust that Catholics should have to pay a double tax for education, — one imposed by law for the public schools, and the other by conscience for the parochial schools. Dr. Power called a meeting of the trustees of the city Churches, who discussed the matter. At their suggestion, he went to Albany and found even the governor, William H. Seward, in favour of the Catholic claims. He even spoke of them favourably in his annual message. It was, however, judged wiser to petition the Common Council of the city, than the legislature of the State. The petition was sent, but the Common Council rejected it. Meetings of the Catholics were held in the city to further the object of the petition ; but, eventually, small, self-seeking ward-politicians, who have ever been the bane of Catholic movements in our cities, got control of these assemblies, and injured rather than helped the cause of Catholic education and of the parochial schools.

When the bishop saw the condition of things, he at once assumed the leadership of the movement. On the second day after his return, one of these meetings was held. He went to it, and told the people that he had taken measures "that all politics should be excluded." He made a masterly speech, dethroned the politicians, and was at once recognized by both priests and people as their leader in furthering a measure which being of a purely religious character was above party politics. "Politics," said he, "must not be introduced : first, for the perhaps insignificant reason that if they be introduced I disappear from among you ; and, secondly, for the very important one that your prospects would thereby be defeated. If you have any regard then for my feelings or your own interests, do not introduce politics. We do not meet for political purposes. I defy our enemies or our friends to show that one word of politics was ever tolerated in our meetings. I trust, therefore, that it will be after I have received notice to retire, that politics will be introduced." The bishop was always present and spoke at the meetings which were held every fortnight in the basement of St. James's Church. On August 10 he published an address of the Roman Catholics to their fellow-citizens of the City and State of New York. In this document copious reasons for the opposition of Catholics to the public schools were given. The following is the strongest part of the document, as written by the bishop: —

"Besides the introduction of the Holy Scriptures without note or comment, with the prevailing theory that from these even children are to get their notions of religion, contrary to our principles, there are in the class-books of those schools false (as we believe) historical statements respecting the men and things of past times, calculated to fill the minds of our children with errors of fact, and at the same time to excite in them prejudice against the religion of their parents and guardians. These passages were not considered as sectarian, in as much as they had been selected as reading lessons, and were not in favour of any particular sect, but merely against the Catholics. We feel it is unjust that such passages should be taught at all in schools to the support of which we are contributors as well as others. But that such books should be put into the hands of our own children, and that, in part, at our own expense, was in our opinion unjust, unnatural, and at all events to us intolerable. Accordingly through very great additional sacrifices, we have been obliged to provide schools, under our churches and elsewhere, in which to educate our children as our conscientious duty required. This we have done, to the number of some thousands, for several years past, during all of which time we have been obliged to pay taxes; and we feel it unjust and oppressive that while we educate our children as well, we contend, as they would be at the public schools, we are denied our portion of the school fund, simply because we, at the same time, endeavour to train them up in principles of virtue and religion. This we feel to be unjust and unequal, for we pay taxes in proportion to our numbers, as other citizens.

"We are supposed to be from one hundred thousand to two hundred thousand in the State. And although most of us are poor, still the poorest man among us is obliged to pay taxes, from the sweat of his brow, in the rent of his room or little tenement. Is it not, then, unjust and hard that such a man cannot have the benefit of education for his child without sacrificing the rights of his religion and conscience? He sends his child to a school, under the protection of the Church, in which these rights will be secure; but he has to support the public school also. In Ireland, he was compelled to support a Church hostile to his religion, and here he is compelled to support schools in which his religion fares but little better, and to support his own school besides.

"Is this the state of things, fellow-citizens, and especially Americans, — is this the state of things worthy of you, worthy of our country, worthy of our just and glorious constitution? Put yourself in the poor man's place, and say whether you would not despise him if he did not labour by every lawful means to emancipate himself from this bondage? He has to pay double taxation for the education of his child, — one to the misinterpreted law of the land, and another to his conscience. He sees his child going to school with perhaps the fragment of a worn-out book, the child, thinly clad, and its bare feet on the frozen pavement; whereas, if he had his rights he could improve the clothing, he could get better books, and have his child better taught than it is possible under actual circumstances.

"Nothing can be more false than some statements of our motives which have been put forth against us. It has been asserted that we seek our share of the school funds for the support and advance of our religion. We beg to assure you with respect, that we would scorn to support or advance our religion at any other than our own expense. But we are unwilling to pay taxes for the purpose of destroying our religion in the minds of our children. This points out the sole difference between what we seek and what some narrow-minded or misinformed journals have accused us of seeking.

"The cold indifference with which it is required that all religion shall be treated in those schools; the Scriptures without note or comment; the selection of passages as reading lessons from Protestant and prejudiced authors on points in which our creed is supposed to be involved; the comments of the teacher, of which the commissioners cannot be cognizant; the school libraries, stuffed with sectarian works against us, — form against our religion a combination of influences prejudicial to our religion, and to whose action it would be criminal in us to expose our children at such an age."

A few weeks later he sent to the Board of Aldermen of New York a petition containing the substance of this address, and asked a share of the school funds for eight parochial schools then flourishing in the city. The Public School Society strongly opposed him, and sent a "Remonstrance" in opposition to the Catholics' petition. The Methodist clergy objected in a body; and the Press raised the cry of "No Popery." The bishop, nothing daunted, appeared before the aldermen to plead in person for what he considered "the cause of the poor and the oppressed." A lawyer was engaged to help him, but became ill, and the bishop had to fight the battle alone. He was opposed by two prominent lawyers, Theodore Sedgwick and Hiram Ketchum, who represented the corporation then known as "The Public School Society." The Rev. Drs. Bond, Bangs, and Reese appeared for the Methodists; Rev. Dr. Spring for the Presbyterians; and Rev. Dr. Knox for the Dutch Reformed. All the sects were united in opposing the Catholic claims. On the day of the debate the City Hall was thronged by crowds of citizens deeply interested in the discussion. When the "Remonstrance" of the Public School Society and of the Methodists had been read, Bishop Hughes rose and in a speech which lasted three hours, dissected the arguments of his opponents, and eloquently urged the justice of the Catholic cause. Mr. Sedgwick and Mr. Ketchum sharply replied. On September 30 the debate was resumed. Doctors Bond, Reese, Knox, Bangs, and Spring, in prepared speeches, attacked the Catholic petition. All the Protestant churches were up in arms and sustained the Public School Society. The reverend gentlemen, instead of confining themselves to the subject of discussion, travelled over the whole field of theological controversy, and raked out of the buried past every charge that could be made against the Catholic Church. The bishop in reply was obliged to follow them. He had no time for preparation, yet in a masterly speech of three hours and a half, with a vehemence and a force and a logic never surpassed, he fought for his creed, refuted the charges against it, urged again the justice of the Catholic petition, and concluded amid a storm of applause in which even his enemies joined. The Public School Society began to feel that its position was untenable. It offered to compromise, agreed to submit the school books to the bishop for expurgation, and even to buy the parochial schools built by the Catholics. But the bishop would not accept the terms or their compromise. He determined to sacrifice nothing. He did not however gain the object of his petition. It was rejected on Jan. 12, 1841, by the Committee of the Board of Aldermen; and the whole board, with one exception, confirmed the action of its committee.

The bishop then called a meeting of Catholics to be held in Washington Hall on February 11. The hall was crowded with an enthusiastic audience, which cheered the bishop as he entered. He made a speech in which he called attention to the narrow-mindedness of the Board of Aldermen. He urged the appointment of a committee to present a memorial to the legislature. This was done and the memorial was presented to Hon. John C. Spencer, Secretary of State and *ex-officio* superintendent of public schools. This official reported his views soon after, and recommended to the legislature a change in the school system of New York City. This change was intended to destroy the sectarian character of the corporation known as the " Public School Society of New York," to weaken its power, to abridge its privileges, and bring it directly under the control of the people of the city. The change was a step toward the present public school system of the State.

This controversy brought the bishop into friendly relations with Governor Seward, a broad-minded and liberal statesman who held the Catholic views as to the necessity of Christian education, and with Mr. Thurlow Weed, afterward a distinguished politician of the Republican party. Bishop Hughes's friendship with these men, and the active part which he took in the " School Question," was the occasion of his being accused of meddling in politics and of being a political intriguer. This, however, he never was. But the politicians, and particularly the professional

"Catholic" politicians, who saw and dreaded the hold which he had acquired over the masses of the people, thought to deter him from the use of his power by calling him a politician. They misrepresented his simplest actions. He had to go to Albany to administer Confirmation the day after the debate in the Common Council, and from Albany to Troy to visit the Churches there. When he returned to New York, he found that a story was circulated that he had been dining with the aldermen, and that some of them had made a bargain with him to vote for the Catholic petition, provided he would go to Albany and get the Catholics to vote against Governor Seward.

In spite of defeat, the bishop did not cease from his crusade in favour of Christian education.

On the 16th, 17th, and 21st of June, in Carroll Hall, he made three speeches reviewing Mr. Ketchum's argument and the objections of the Public School Society against the Catholic petition. Among the audience on these occasions were Lieutenant-Governor Bradish and many of the State senators.

The question was brought before the Senate at Albany and there hotly debated. The Catholic claims were assailed by every argument that prejudice or bigotry could suggest. The Press helped the rich and powerful Public School Society. The "Journal of Commerce," on the day before the subject was to come up in the Senate, published a long screed containing all the old charges against "Popery," and among them the fictitious bull of excommunication which Sterne, as a joke, inserted in "Tristram Shandy." The agent of the Public School Society placed on the desk of each senator a copy of this paper with the article marked. The calumny was successful. The senators were frightened and postponed the vote on the memorial until January, 1842. Thus even the strongest minds are sometimes frightened away from the path of justice by the scarecrow of an old calumny.

CHAPTER VIII.

CLOSE OF THE SCHOOL CONTROVERSY.

WHILE the Catholics were being assailed in the Press and in the legislature, for presuming to protest against the sectarian monopoly known as the "Public School Society," the bishop continued his work among the Churches of his diocese, administering confirmation and fostering charities for the protection of orphans and waifs; but he did not discontinue his warfare against the rich school monopoly in the city. The question had now become one of politics as well as one of religion. A political contest was forced upon him against his will or his inclinations. The organs of the Public School Society had tried, previous to the fall election, to inflame the minds of Protestant voters against him. He was denounced as a Jesuit, an intriguer, opposed to free institutions, to a Republican form of government, and the foe of " free schools, the palladium of our liberties." All the clap-trap nonsense of the unfrocked monk or of the expelled nun who had been sent away from her convent, all the stale calumnies of the past, were daily published by so-called respectable newspapers, and used as lawful weapons against the "Romish" bishop. Candidates for office were threatened; they were compelled to pledge themselves to vote against granting the Catholic petition. Every attempt was made to frighten even the bishop. His life was menaced; anonymous writers made menaces; the Press was full of denunciation, and spread-eagle orators hurled anathemas at him from the stump. But his courage rose higher with every attack. His answer to all the threats was an attempt to form a distinct Catholic party. The time was short before the elections, but he would try to influence them.

Consequently, on October 29, four days before the election, the bishop called his people to meet him, at Carroll Hall. They came in crowds, and at his suggestion nominated a full list of candidates friendly to the Catholic petition. He made an eloquent speech in favour of the ticket. He never was more in earnest; all his powers were roused to the highest pitch. "Now," said he, in calm, deliberate tones that increased in volume as he spoke, "if you are unanimously determined to convince this community that you are in earnest, that you sincerely feel that there is a *bona-fide* grievance of which you complain, you will support the candidates thus offered for your choice; because if you do not, you have no alternative left but that of voting for the declared enemies of your rights. You have often voted for others, and they did not vote for you; but now you are determined to uphold with your own votes your own rights. Will you then stand by the rights of your offspring, who have so long suffered under the operation of this injurious system? Will you adhere to the nominations made?" The answer was loud cheers and cries of, "We will! we will!" "Will you be united?" At this point the whole audience rose to their feet, cheered, waved handkerchiefs, and cried out that they would stand by him to the last. "Will you let all men see that you are worthy sons of the nation to which you belong?" "Never fear; we will! We will till death!" was the answer. "Will none of you flinch?" he cried with emphasis and flashing eye. The reply to this question was a great shout of, "We will not!" The people, wild with excitement, rose and cheered so long and so loud that he could not continue his speech for several minutes. "I care not for party men," he cried, with a contemptuous wave of the hand; "bring them to the test, and you find great promises, lean performances. It is time that you should convince them that you are not the pliant body they mistake you to be. You will have nothing to do with the men who go to the Senate and Assembly pledged to act against you?" "No, no, no! That we won't!" replied the audience. "I ask then," said he, in conclusion, "once for all, — and with the answer let the meeting close, — will this meeting pledge its honour, as the representative of the portion of our oppressed community for whom I have so often pleaded, here as elsewhere, — will it pledge its honour that it will stand by these candidates whose names have been read, and that no man composing this vast audience will ever vote for any one pledged to oppose our just claims and incontrovertible rights!" The meeting pledged itself as he wished, and then adjourned.

Of course the politicians trembled, fretted, and raved at the bishop's actions. They felt that a master-mind and a master-hand was at work, — a man who despised trickery, who had courage enough to expose it, and force enough to trample on it. They were jealous of the hold he had on the affections of the Catholic population. He could sway them as he willed, and no one since or before has ever had such power over them.

The politicians abused him for violating what they called the laws of "propriety;" although they habitually violated laws more important than those of propriety. From 1840 to 1844 Bishop Hughes was the most popular, and at the same time the best abused, man in the United States. He was popular with all good and fair-minded citizens, unpopular with the dishonest, the untruthful, and the bigoted.

When the election came off in November, the politicians were amazed to find that the "Catholic" party, although it had no time for perfect organization, polled two thousand two hundred votes. This result showed that the Catholics, if properly managed, would act independently in regard to any question which affected their rights or their consciences. Their vote was very large considering that their ticket had been only four days in the field. Governor Seward, always friendly to the Catholic claims, had been attacked for his sympathy with them. He wrote to Bishop Hughes, a few days after the election: —

"It is your fortune as well as mine that philanthropic conceptions for the improvement of society come in conflict with existing interests founded in existing prejudices. I have noticed several very gratifying indications of a determination among your people to vindicate and sustain you. If this should be the case, you will see henceforth a rapid transition among the people at large. The session of the legislature approaches. I will say to you, with all freedom, that I propose to assert my opinions and principles with firmness, and to submit the subject of the educational system to the direct action of the legislature. May I not hope that your concern on that great subject will induce you to accede to my wishes by making me a brief visit before the close of navigation?"

Some of the professional politicians of New York, who then as now had the name of being Catholics without being so in reality, tried to turn public opinion against the bishop; but the true Catholics of his diocese stood stoutly by him. They held a meeting in Washington Hall, November 16, at which they expressed their "unwavering confidence in his zeal, judgment, and acknowledged ability," and testified "to the respect which his fearless, independent, and judicious course in relation to the subject of education had excited in their minds."

Governor Seward, true to his promise, urged the school question on the attention of the legislature, in his message of January, 1842. Some of the politicians became at once alarmed. It was rumoured that the Irish Catholics were deserting the *Loco-foco* party and would go over to the Whigs. Some of the newspapers charged the bishop with attempting to form a Catholic party in politics; but he had no such intention, although the school question continued to be agitated. At length the legislature attempted to compromise, and for this purpose abolished the old school system and established a new one of a less sectarian character. Yet the compromise was a failure, and has never satisfied Catholics. Their claim has always been for distinctly religious education in the school, and that education belongs to the parents and not to the State. When the State assumes the rôle of a schoolmaster, it usurps parental rights, assumes spiritual functions, and interferes with the conscience of the individual.

In the fall elections of this year a riot took place at the polls in the sixth ward. An anti-Catholic mob marched to the bishop's house in Mulberry Street, broke his windows, and ran away; fortunately for the mob the bishop was out of town. Had he been at home and heard of their coming, they would have had a warm reception.

The old Public School Society died after a fight of two years with the bishop, and the schools under its control passed over to the management of the new Board of Education. The bishop, although not satisfied with the half victory which he had won, thought it wiser to discontinue the controversy, and set about building up a system of parochial schools sustained by the voluntary contributions of the faithful. In 1843 he convoked the priests of Brooklyn and New York, in the cathedral in Mulberry Street, and read to them an address in which he urged them to redouble their efforts "to diffuse true education among the children of their flocks."

He had already tried to give an impetus to higher Catholic education. In 1840 he had removed the ecclesiastical seminary from Lafargeville to Fordham, where St. John's College was opened in June, 1841. He bought the estate of Rose Hill, at Fordham, where the college is, for thirty thousand dollars. The first president of this college was Rev. John McCloskey, afterward Cardinal-Archbishop of New York. In

1841, Bishop Hughes brought over from France a colony of the Ladies of the Sacred Heart, who founded, at Manhattanville, an academy whose branches have since spread through the city and State. The first superioress of the Manhattanville Academy was Madame Elizabeth Galitzin, a Russian princess, and cousin of Prince Demetrius Augustine Galitzin, who became a priest, gave up home and country, and spent years in missionary labours among the Alleghany Mountains. The Galitzins were born in St. Petersburg, and were converts from the Russian Church.

The bishop also made about this time an unsuccessful effort to bring over a colony of "Christian Brothers" from Ireland to assume control of the parochial male schools of the diocese. The controversy on the school question had made him realize more fully than ever the necessity of good Catholic schools, both for the poor and for the rich, and he bent all his energies to give his flock the full benefit of a sound Christian education.

CHAPTER IX.

FIRST DIOCESAN SYNOD OF NEW YORK. — THE CONTROVERSY WITH DAVID HALE AND THE TRUSTEES OF ST. LOUIS CHURCH, BUFFALO. — BISHOP MCCLOSKEY APPOINTED COADJUTOR. — THE NATIVE AMERICAN EXCITEMENT, AND MAYOR HARPER.

IN 1841 there was a debt of $300,000 on the ten Catholic Churches of New York City. This was considered at that time a very heavy debt. It was not equally distributed. St. Peter's, in Barclay Street, had so large a share of it that the corporation was almost bankrupt. The bishop was annoyed by this condition of affairs, and thought to remedy it by trying to unite all the Catholics of the city into an organization for the payment of the Church debts, and thus to relieve the parishes that were in the greatest financial danger. The Catholic population of the city was then from sixty to eighty thousand souls. The bishop called a meeting of them in Carroll Hall, on May 3, 1841, and proposed the plan of a "Church Debt Association." Seven of the ten Churches joined it; and in the course of a year $17,000 were collected by the society. But the masses of the people had no zeal in the enterprise; so at the end of the year the association was disbanded, leaving many of the Churches still heavily embarrassed.

On the 29th of August of the same year he convoked the first Catholic Synod of New York. The clergy met at the cathedral, and during three days' deliberation enacted many laws, some of them against hasty marriages and secret societies. The secret societies which entrapped the poor Irish emigrants, and divided them into factions hostile to one another, were specially condemned and denounced. These societies were numerous among the railroad labourers, then chiefly Irish, throughout the country, and took names from the different provinces of Ireland. The "Far Downs," the "Corkonians," and the "Connaughtmen," as some of these quarrelsome societies were called, although shunned and abhorred by the better class of labourers, brought much disgrace to the Catholic-Irish name. The synod was chiefly instrumental in destroying these pests. It also completely abolished the lay-trustee system and made the rector of the church the master of it, in temporals as well as in spirituals. Some of the secular newspapers attacked the bishop for the law against the lay-trustees, and called it an infringement on the rights of the laity. The bishop answered his assailants in a strong letter to "David Hale, Esq., who is some kind of a Presbyterian; M. M. Noah, Esq., who is a Jew; and the editor (whose name I do not know) of a little paper called the 'Aurora.'" Mr. Hale, who was then the editor of the New York "Journal of Commerce," replied to the bishop, and exchanged three controversial letters with him.

Only one board of trustees in the whole diocese refused to obey the enactment against them. This was the board of St. Louis' Church, Buffalo. The bishop at once withdrew the priest from the church; the trustees petitioned for a pastor. The bishop's answer was characteristic: —

"You have destroyed the peace and respectability of your congregation; you have annoyed your pastor until he felt himself obliged to leave you; you have attempted to injure the character of your bishop, by authorizing the publication of falsehoods and calumnies against him in the newspapers, — and in the midst of all this you ask me for a priest! You shall not govern your bishop, but your bishop shall govern you in all ecclesiastical matters. When you are willing to walk in the way of your holy faith, as your forefathers did, and be numbered among the flock of the diocese, precisely as all other trustees and congregations are, then I shall send you a priest, if I should have one."

The trustees finally obeyed, and confessed their fault in a public document written by himself and printed in the newspapers. When the rebels had thus atoned for their sin, he opened their church and gave them a priest. But when the diocese was divided, and Father Timon became Bishop of Buffalo, the trouble broke out again. In consequence of this disturbance the Church Property Bill of 1855 was passed by the New York Legislature.

In the autumn of 1842 Bishop Hughes visited the northern and western parts of the State, and had opportunities of displaying the wonderful activity and physical strength which distinguished him. Thus he arrived at Binghamton late of a Saturday night; the next day he administered confirmation, preached four times, and dedicated a church. Although fatigued, on the Monday following he preached twice, and consecrated a graveyard. On Tuesday he rode thirty miles, in an open wagon, to a place called Oxford, where he preached, and the evening of the same day he started for Utica. Such labours as these undermined his fine constitution; he grew sick, and felt that he needed help in the work of his diocese. Consequently, in May, 1843, at the Fifth Council of Baltimore, he asked the assembled prelates for a coadjutor. They recommended to the Holy See for that office Rev. John McCloskey, then rector of St. Joseph's Church in Sixth Avenue, New York City. After the Council, the bishop went to Europe with a financial plan which he hoped to realize in Belgium. He proposed to negotiate there a three or four per cent loan on the consolidated debts of his diocese, and pay off all the American mortgages which were running at a higher rate of interest.

On Wednesday, June 7, he left New York on the ship "George Washington," in the company of his old friend Bishop Purcell of Cincinnati, Father De Smet, the great Jesuit Indian missionary, and Mr. Thurlow Weed. The ship was becalmed near the coast of Cork, so that they all landed there and travelled overland to Dublin. The spot where they went ashore on the Irish coast was near the little village of Courtmacsherry. They were taken for French officers and emissaries by the English officials of the place. With some difficulty the American travellers proved their true character, continued their journey, and reached Dublin on the eve of a great " Repeal of the Union" meeting at Donnybrook. The bishop, with Father De Smet, attended the meeting, where they met Daniel O'Connell. Then the bishop and his fellow-passengers went to Liverpool, where an amusing incident took place which Mr. Weed used to relate with pleasure. Some one had given the bishop two bottles of snuff, which the custom-house officials found in his trunk, and for which they charged him four dollars' duty.

"You must pay this, sir," said the officer, "in honour of the Queen."

"For which I should like to give her Majesty a *pinch*," replied the bishop.

His financial scheme fell through, as no Belgian capitalist would invest in his *Emprunt Catholique de*

New York; but instead of money he obtained several priests to work in the missions of his diocese. He returned to New York in October, and in the following December we find him lecturing to an audience of thirty-five hundred people, on " The Mixture of Civil and Ecclesiastical Power in the Middle Ages." In February, 1844, he lectured every Thursday evening in his cathedral on doctrinal subjects, before very large audiences.

On March 10, 1844, Rev. John McCloskey was consecrated as his coadjutor, with the title of Bishop of Axiern, *in partibus infidelium.* Two other priests of New York were made bishops at the same time: the Rev. Andrew Byrne, Bishop of Little Rock, Arkansas, and the Rev. William Quarter, Bishop of Chicago. The consecrators were Bishop Hughes, Bishop Whelan, of Richmond, afterward of Wheeling, and Bishop Fenwick, of Boston.

It was in this year that the so-called " Native American " political party became conspicuous by creating riots and otherwise disturbing the peace of the country. They singled out Bishop Hughes, because of his prominence and aggressiveness, for special abuse. They misrepresented his conduct and his purposes; their newspapers attacked him daily. His controversy on the " School Question " was distorted into an attempt to drive the Bible out of the public schools. He was accused of leading an Irish Catholic party in an attempt to get control of the government. His overthrow of the lay-trustees was misrepresented as an effort to establish a despotic priestcraft hostile to the spirit of American liberty. The "Native American" orators, and some of the newspapers, denounced him as an ambitious foe of republican institutions and a satellite of the Pope. In Philadelphia, a school controversy similar to the one in New York had arisen, and was the occasion of much excitement, which spread over the country. Bishop Hughes advised his flock to keep quiet, and to do nothing to provoke the prejudices of the political faction which was abusing the name of "American." He foresaw that the smoke of prejudice would soon be dissipated, and that the flames of bigotry would soon die out. He counted on the good sense and the sober judgment of the majority of American citizens. The Catholics, generally, followed their pastor's counsel, although some of them fretted under abuse which they knew to be unmerited. On the night of the municipal election in 1844, a mob of over a thousand "Native Americans," yelling, groaning, cursing, and bearing "No Popery" banners, marched through the sixth and the fourteenth, then called the "Irish," wards of the city. Yet so docile to the bishop's advice were the people of his faith, though naturally an impulsive and pugnacious race, that not one of them resented the insult. But although the bishop was patient, he was not a coward. He would not permit his Church or his person to be attacked with impunity. His armour was always on, and his lance always couched for a foe. He was a natural-born soldier. When, therefore, he heard that a threat had been made to burn down his cathedral, he caused three or four thousand of the most intelligent and prominent Catholics to arm themselves, and to take possession of the churchyard in Mott Street, and defend the building. When the " Natives " heard of these preparations, they were afraid to attack, and no more was heard of the threat.

So heated were minds at that time that a lie of a few lines, in anti-Catholic newspapers, was capable of exciting the most fearful riots. In Philadelphia, the " Natives " destroyed St. Michael's Church and St. Augustine's Church and Rectory, the valuable library of the Augustinians, as well as the residence of the Sisters of Charity, and a number of houses inhabited by Irish families. In fact, such was the danger of mob-violence that public worship had to be suspended in all the Catholic Churches of that city. The news of these outrages roused the martial blood and the indignation of the bishop. Had he lived in Philadelphia, he would have resisted the mobs with an armed body; he would have roused his people, and if they were to be murdered, he would not let them die unavenged. In the midst of the excitement, some one advised him to issue a pastoral urging the Catholics to keep the peace. But he argued, Catholics have not broken the peace; they have kept it too well in Philadelphia. They should have defended their property. He declared publicly, and with an emphasis that all could understand, that if a "single Catholic Church were burned in New York, the city would become a second Moscow." Some of the city officials begged him to restrain the Irish, who were excited by what had been done in the neighbouring city. "I have not the power," was his reply; "you must take care that they are not provoked." He blamed the Catholics of Philadelphia for their lack of organization. "They should have defended their Churches," said he, "since the authorities could not, or would not, do it for them. We might forbear harming the intruder into our *house*, until the last; but his first violence to our Church should be promptly and decisively repelled."

He made preparations for war; he garrisoned every Catholic Church in the city with an armed force of one or two thousand men "resolved after taking as many lives as they could in defense of their property, to give up, if necessary, their own lives for the same cause." But he warned his people against making the first attack, and they obeyed him like trained soldiers. Some of them were so determined to make every resistance, that they would have set fire to their own houses and destroyed the city, if any mob had ventured to attack them. They felt as if they were surrounded by enemies. The very officials that should protect them were in league against them; so they were resolved to protect themselves and their Churches, and to stand by their bishop to the death. Through the "Freeman's Journal," his organ, he addressed his people. Having heard that a band of "Natives" were coming from Philadelphia, bearing an American flag which they lyingly said had been trampled on by "savage foreigners;" and that the New York "Know-Nothings" were to escort their visiting brethren through the city, and hold a meeting in City Hall Park, he foresaw that the result would be a riot and bloodshed. He consequently issued an extra edition of the "Freeman," in which he warned Catholics to keep away from all public meetings and give no cause for provocation to the "Church-burners, convent-sackers, and grave-robbers." He called also on the mayor, Robert H. Morris, and urged him to prevent the "Know-Nothing" meeting.

"Are you afraid," said the mayor, "that some of your churches will be burned?"

"No, sir; but I am afraid that some of yours will be burned? We can protect our own. I come to warn you for your own good."

"Do you think, Bishop, that your people would attack the procession?"

"I do not; but the 'Native Americans' want to provoke a Catholic riot, and if they can do it in no other way, I believe they would not scruple to attack the procession themselves, for the sake of making it appear that the Catholics had assailed them."

"What then would you have me do?"

"I did not come to tell you what to do. I am a Churchman, not the Mayor of New York; but if I were the mayor, I would examine the laws of the State, and see if there were not attached to the police force a battery of artillery, and a company or so of infantry, and a squadron of horse; and I think I should find that there were; and if so I should order them out." He also advised Mayor Morris to see the "Know-Nothing" mayor-elect, Mr. Harper, and get him to use his influence with his supporters to prevent a riot.

The bishop's firm action prevented a disturbance of the peace; his advice was taken. No riot was attempted. Even later in July, when riots broke out again in the city of "Brotherly Love," the New York "Know-Nothings" were quiet. They were afraid of the fighting bishop; and they knew that he would meet force with force. But cowards who were afraid to fight him openly, assailed him privately. He received several anonymous letters, one of which threatened him with assassination. It afforded him occasion for a public letter published on May 17,

1844, in the "Courier and Enquirer." In this document he answers all his assailants. He gives a full account of his life, refutes the slanders of some newspapers which had falsely charged him with disloyalty to American institutions, and strongly attacks the New York "Herald" and the "Commercial Advertiser" for circulating calumnies against him. He always felt keenly any attack on his loyalty as a citizen, or on the loyalty of the Church of which he was a representative. He resented any statement or imputation that there was anything in the Catholic religion which was not reconcilable with the fullest American political liberty. The charge of disloyalty was the special charge of the "Native Americans."[1] He refuted it again and again, only to see the same old falsehood repeated by the enemies of his faith. His own conduct proved that a more devoted son of the republic never lived, and that his intense love of the Church only made his patriotism the stronger.

[1] I have sometimes called this political faction "The Know-Nothings," because their aim and motive were the same as those of the "Know-Nothings," ten years later; I believe, however, that historically the name "Know-Nothing" was not in general use until 1854.

CHAPTER X.

HE VISITS EUROPE IN THE INTEREST OF EDUCATION. — HIS POLITICAL OPINIONS. — ORGANIZATION OF THE SISTERS OF CHARITY IN HIS DIOCESE. — SYMPATHY WITH THE IRISH PATRIOTS OF 1848. — HIS CONTROVERSY WITH "KIRWAN."

THE bishop, as we have seen, was not satisfied with the exclusively secular education of the public schools. He had also given up the hope that a concession would be made by the school authorities to satisfy the conscience of Catholics who insisted on the union of religious and secular education in the school. He therefore formed the resolution to establish a school in every parish of his diocese. For this, however, teachers were needed. He determined to seek them in Europe, and consequently on March 19, 1845, he crossed the ocean and brought over a colony of "Christian Brothers," — a body of laymen consecrated by vow to the education of boys, — and a number of Sisters of Mercy, to take charge of an orphan asylum and of hospitals to be erected. He returned to New York, April 21, 1846. In July of the same year he sold St. John's College at Fordham to the Jesuit Fathers, some of whom came from Kentucky to take charge of it. The college had been previously chartered in April, 1846, and enjoyed all the privileges of a university. So flourishing was it that in July, 1846, there were one hundred and forty-six students in it. Its debt was then forty thousand dollars. He did not, however, sell St. Joseph's seminary with the college; but the Jesuits, at his request, taught the seminarists until A. D. 1855. At the Sixth Council of Baltimore, in May, 1846, he asked for a division of his diocese. The Fathers of the Council acceded to his request; and two new sees were erected in the State of New York, one at Albany, the other at Buffalo. In July, 1847, Rev. John McCloskey was appointed Bishop of Albany, and the Rev. John Timon, Bishop of Buffalo.

The Mexican War had just begun, and our secretary of state, Hon. James Buchanan, at the suggestion of the President, thought that Bishop Hughes would be a good envoy to send from our Government to Mexico. Hence an invitation from the secretary was sent to the bishop, asking him to come to Washington to advise with the President on "public affairs of importance." The bishop, who was then at the Baltimore Council, consulted the other bishops as to the propriety of accepting such an office. They advised him to refuse it, unless President Polk would give him the full rank and title of an ambassador.

He went to Washington, where Mr. Buchanan first consulted him about the appointment of Catholic chaplains in the army, and then spoke about the embassy. But the President could not give the bishop the full rank of an envoy, because the Mexican Government had just refused to receive the American minister duly accredited. And so the affair ended.

The bishop was even then on terms of intimacy with many of our prominent statesmen, who admired his genius. He felt at home in their company. Although he never voted but once or twice, and never tried to influence a vote except in the school controversy, he had a taste for political discussion. He knew the arguments of the different parties well, and understood the wants of the country and the rivalries of the different sections of it. He was a shrewd judge of politicians and of their plans and purposes. Among them he was combative in conversation, but not rashly aggressive. He never began the attack, but he never avoided it. He was conscious of all his powers, and felt that no antagonist was his superior. In 1852 he voted the Whig ticket for Henry Clay, just because, as he said, some of his congregation threatened him if he would not vote for the Democratic candidate. When Mr. Clay afterward visited New York, the bishop called on him at his hotel. The moment Mr. Clay received his card, he turned out all his other distinguished guests, hastened to greet the bishop, and spent an hour with him in private conversation.

From political questions, the bishop now turned to purely ecclesiastical affairs, which gave him great annoyance. The Sisters of Charity in his diocese were a branch of the order founded at Emmittsburg, Maryland, by Mother Seton. They were not under the control of the bishop, but were governed by a mother superioress who lived at Emmittsburg. This state of affairs never pleased him; yet he would have probably made no change if orders which disarranged his plans had not been sent to them by their superioress. He wished the Sisters in his diocese to take charge of orphan boys, although this was contrary to the Emmittsburg rule. But the Sisters in New York, considering the necessities of the case, had hitherto obeyed the bishop. Their clerical superior was a Sulpitian priest, Rev. Mr. Deluol, who lived in Baltimore. He finally ordered the Sisters to withdraw from the male orphan asylums in New York. The bishop protested, and succeeded with difficulty in getting a concession that all the Sisters who desired should remain in his diocese and organize themselves into a separate community under diocesan control. Thirty-one out of fifty Sisters joined the new society, which became known as the "Sisters of Charity of St. Vincent de Paul." The Emmittsburg Sisters, soon afterward becoming affiliated to the community founded in

France by St. Vincent de Paul, adopted the French dress and discipline. The New York Sisters, whose mother house is Mount St. Vincent on the Hudson, retained the old constitution and the dress adopted by Mother Seton.

Having thus summarily settled this case, and put the orphans of his diocese under the charge of Sisters obedient to himself, his mind was diverted to an entirely different affair. In 1848 an ill-advised and badly-planned insurrection broke out in Ireland. The news stirred the bishop's blood. Although, as he said, "he was so much identified with all that is American that he had almost forgotten his foreign birth," yet the welfare of his native land always excited his interest. The wrongs of Ireland had made him hate English rule. He grieved over the famine which, in 1847, had decimated the Irish people. When he heard of it, he stopped the order for a collection for his theological seminary, and ordered one for the famine-stricken Irish instead. "It is better that seminaries should be suspended," said he, "than that so large a portion of our fellow-beings should be exposed to death by starvation." He collected fourteen thousand dollars, and sent this sum to Ireland for the relief of the sufferers; he also delivered a lecture for their benefit. The title of it showed the animus of the orator, "The Tyrant and his Famine, or the Irish Tragedy of Six Hundred

Years." He further showed his sympathy with the insurrection in Ireland by accompanying Horace Greeley to a public meeting in its favour, held in Vauxhall Garden on August 14, 1848. On that occasion he said: —

"There may be a crisis in the history of a nation which will authorize and almost require one in my station to depart from what may be considered the ordinary and legitimate routine of his official duties; I think that such a crisis and such a period have arrived in the history of Ireland. By the last news it appears that the oppressor and his victim stand face to face. I come among you, gentlemen, not as an advocate of war, it would ill accord with my profession; my office is properly to be a peacemaker, when it is possible. But I come in the name of sacred humanity, not, if you will, to put arms into the hands of men by which they may destroy the lives of others, but to give my voice and my mite to shield the unprotected bosoms of the sons of Ireland. It is not for me to say anything calculated to excite your feelings, when, as you can perceive, I can scarcely repress my own. My object in coming here was to show you that in my conscience I have no scruples in aiding the cause in every way worthy a patriot and a Christian."

At this meeting he contributed five hundred dollars "to purchase a shield to interpose between the oppressor and the victim." He had no sympathy, however, with the party which had helped to thwart O'Connell in his efforts to obtain Home Rule for

Ireland by constitutional methods. He saw that the attempt of the Young Ireland party to separate Ireland totally from England, would be a failure and result only in the useless shedding of blood. Many of the young Irelanders were tainted with irreligion: French radicalism had corrupted their minds. Consequently he opposed their plans; and when they came to America, he was obliged to reprove some of their leaders. One of these, a very able and accomplished orator and writer who afterward repented of his radicalism, Thomas D'Arcy McGee, of the New York "Nation," charged the priests and the bishops with being the cause of the failure of the Irish rebellion. It is true that the majority of the clergy of Ireland did oppose the insurrection, because they saw the utter impossibility of its success. The bishop thus replied to McGee in an article in the "Freeman's Journal," "The clergy would have been faithless to the obligations of religion and of humanity, if they had not interposed, seeing, as they must have seen, the certain and inevitable consequence of a movement so nobly conceived, but so miserably conducted." He described the disciples of the McGee school as an "Irish tribe whose hearts have apostatized from the honoured creed of their country, but whose lips have not yet mustered the bad courage to disavow the faith of their forefathers." He also exposed the plans and denounced the conduct of the Red Republicans who at this time were disturbing the public peace by revolt and rebellion all over Europe.

About the middle of December, 1848, Pius IX. was driven by them from Rome. On the Sunday following the bishop preached in St. Patrick's Cathedral, on the position of the supreme pontiff, and ordered a collection of Peter pence to be taken up in all the Churches of the New York diocese. The sum collected was nearly seven thousand dollars. One of the Young Ireland papers advised that this sum should be sent to the Pope privately, for fear of offending American ideas of republicanism. The bishop replied to this counsel with his usual frankness. He had nothing to conceal, "The American people," said he, "are wise, sensible, and just; and they despise the man who does not appreciate the first principles of the country in which he lives." In January, 1850, he lectured in Philadelphia upon "The Church and the World since the Accession of Pius IX," and on May 12, following, he caused a solemn Mass of thanksgiving to be celebrated in his cathedral on account of the Pope's return from exile to the Eternal City. On this occasion he preached a sermon strongly denouncing the atheism of the European revolutionists, and defending the right of the Pope to temporal sovereignty. Some of the newspapers attacked the sermon, which he defended in a letter to the "Courier and Enquirer." His contention was that revolution is justifiable only in extreme cases of oppression, and that there was no excuse for the Roman revolution. He showed that the people of the Pope's kingdom were neither overtaxed nor oppressed; and that the revolutionists there were either the paid agents of the King of Sardinia or open atheists hostile to all religion. He denied the parity between our revolution, the Irish rebellion, and that of the Roman insurrection. We had been taxed unjustly, the Irish cruelly oppressed by a foreign power; while the people of Rome were governed by a mild ruler who was one of themselves. "The papal government," he truly wrote, "was paternal, kind, and considerate. The taxes on the people of the Roman States were light; their fidelity to their sovereign unquestioned," until foreign intrigue, bribery, and Sardinian ambition had sown discontent among them.

He preached and wrote incessantly. In December, 1847, he delivered a discourse in the House of Representatives at Washington. His subject was "Christianity the only Source of Moral, Social, and Political Regeneration." The invitation to make this discourse came from the most distinguished statesmen in the country, — from John Quincy Adams, Stephen A. Douglas, John C. Calhoun, Mr. Benton, and others. He believed that our republic would not be safe unless it remained Christian; and he believed that Catholic

Christianity, as being the most conservative, was necessary to the perpetuity of our free institutions. In support of these opinions he wrote a series of articles, in the " Freeman's Journal," "on the importance of being in communion with Christ's one, holy, Catholic, and apostolic Church." These were in part an answer to the Rev. Nicholas Murray, an Irish Presbyterian minister of Elizabeth, New Jersey, who, under a pseudonym, wrote " Kirwan's Letters to Bishop Hughes." When the bishop afterward found out who " Kirwan " was, he wrote six letters, which were published under the name of " Kirwan Unmasked." These letters are models of pure English and good logic. They are among the best productions of the bishop's pen. They are clear, direct, and forcible, and show him to be a master of good English. He handled " Kirwan " with the skill of a trained logician, and exposed him to the contempt of his Irish countrymen as an apostate and an assailer of the faith and race of his Catholic parents.

But while the bishop was thus occupied with literary labour, he neglected none of his other duties. His daily work, which is like the task of every Catholic bishop, is thus described by John R. G. Hassard, in a passage well worth quoting : —

"At home, besides the duties of his ministry, the instruction of neophytes, the supervision of the affairs of all the Churches, the regulation of the finances of the diocese, the satisfaction of heavy debts upon ecclesiastical property, the devising of means for building new churches, the establishment of Catholic schools, the foundation of charitable and religious institutions, he was obliged to carry a load of worry and perplexity which was not entailed on him by his office, but imposed by the selfishness or the egotism or ignorance of persons who had no claim on his attention. His letter-book from the year 1848 down to a period when, from the very multitude of unwarrantable calls upon his time, and from the weight of gathering years, he felt obliged to disregard many of those who addressed him, presents an amusing study. Young men in Ireland whom he never heard of asked his advise about coming to America. One wants a situation in a bank; another inquires about business in general. All sorts of people send him boxes and packages to be forwarded to their relatives in all sorts of out-of-the-way towns in America. Priests in Europe send him restitution-money that has been given them in the confessional by penitent thieves, and beg him to find out (mostly with the vaguest directions) the persons to whom it rightfully belongs. Emigrants send him money, and request him to buy drafts to transmit to their friends in the old country. Poor people in the old country, on the other hand, ask him to find out their emigrant friends, whose address they do not know. A little army of office-seekers besiege him for letters of introduction. Pious souls write him letters of eight pages about their worldly and spiritual troubles. Protestant clergymen, preparing themselves for a terrible assault upon the abominations of Popery, request him to state, as clearly as possible, the Catholic doctrine on this or that question. One gentleman consults him about the Broadway railroad. A great many gentlemen ask for loans of fifty dollars. Suspicious, quarrelsome, or malicious persons trouble him with every kind of absurd charge against their parish priest. Most of these are promptly and politely answered; and in the great majority of cases, an effort is made to comply with their reasonable demands. There was another class of persons who occupied a great deal of his time, but to whom he was always glad to surrender himself, — I mean honest inquirers after Catholic truth. He thought no labour thrown away which was bestowed in explaining to them the doctrines of the Church, or answering their objections. A very great number of persons were led into the Church through his influence or under his instructions."[1]

[1] Life of Archbishop Hughes, p. 319.

CHAPTER XI.

HE IS MADE AN ARCHBISHOP. — THE ERECTION OF NEW SEES. — THE KNOW-NOTHING MOVEMENT OF 1854. — THE FIRST PROVINCIAL COUNCIL OF NEW YORK. — CONTROVERSY WITH ERASTUS BROOKS. — THE CATHOLIC VOTE.

THE Seventh Council of Baltimore, held in May, 1849, had recommended to the Holy See the erection of three new archbishoprics in the United States, — one at New York, another at Cincinnati, and the third at New Orleans. Baltimore, St. Louis, and Oregon City were then the only metropolitan sees in the country. Rome consented; and on Oct. 3, 1850, Bishop Hughes received the brief elevating him to the dignity of an archbishop, with the bishops of Boston, of Hartford, of Albany, and of Buffalo, as his suffragants. On November 10, of the same year, he sailed for Rome. Before his departure he issued a pastoral on the necessity of the religious education of youth. When he arrived in England, he was treated with unusual respect, and at Rome he was invited by the authorities of the English College to assist, with other bishops and many cardinals, in celebrating the feast of Saint Thomas à Becket. During his stay in the Eternal City, in January, 1851, he gave a course of controversial sermons in the Church of St. Andrea delle Frate, and on the following feast of Saint Agatha, February 5, he preached her panegyric before a distinguished audience. Rome had now fully recognized his ability, and the English speaking world was filled with his name. A pamphlet which he had written on "The Decline of Protestantism, and its Causes" was translated into Italian and printed in the Roman newspapers.

The report was even circulated that he was going to be made a cardinal. It originated in Washington, where the government was friendly to him; and the American Minister at Rome urged the matter on the papal court. But Pius IX. objected that there was no vacant hat among the cardinal priests; and some of the American bishops wrote to the Holy See that it was inopportune to make an American cardinal.

The Pope himself conferred the pallium on him on April 3, 1851, and a month later he left Rome for Vienna. On June 11 he sailed from Liverpool for New York, where he landed after a voyage of eleven days. On July 21 the Catholics of New York gave him a banquet at the Astor House.

Immediately on his arrival home he took great interest in the establishment of the Catholic University in Dublin, and gave permission to priests sent from

Ireland to America to collect money for the purpose. Then he engaged in a controversy with the New York "Tribune." This journal had criticised a discourse which he had made attacking Kossuth and certain other European revolutionists. The archbishop showed that they were the enemies of religion, and that their attempted revolution was not justifiable. In a letter to Mr. Greeley, of November 21, he wrote: —

"I deny, with the Catholic Church, any right of one man, by physical coercion, to compel the conscience of another man. Hence, therefore, I am opposed to all penal laws having the coercion of conscience for their object. In countries which are already divided and broken up into religious sects, mutual toleration, kindness, and good-will in all the civil and social relations of life, constitute at once, in my opinion, the duties and the right of all. But I am not aware that a Protestant State, such as Sweden, is bound, by way of granting religious liberty, to place atheism on the same footing as Lutheranism. Neither am I of opinion that the sovereign pontiff, whose subjects are entirely Catholic and united in belief, is bound to throw his States open for the preaching of every form of Protestantism and infidelity."

When Kossuth arrived in New York, the Catholics, warned by the archbishop, would not recognize him. The archbishop showed that the Hungarian revolutionist was only a demagogue, — a fact which slowly found credence in the Protestant community. In

March, 1852, the archbishop gave a lecture on the "Catholic Chapter in the History of the United States." He sent a copy of it to an old Protestant friend of his in Philadelphia, Mr. Biddle. This gentleman, in reply, made many interesting statements. His father had been an officer of rank on the staff of General Washington during the Revolutionary War. Mr. Biddle wrote : —

"My late father often said, that during this contest the rank and file of the best disciplined and most effective continental regiments of the Pennsylvania line were chiefly Irish Catholics; and three of these very religious regiments were commanded by the sons of Irishmen : namely, Wayne, Irvine, and Shea, — the former the distinguished favourite of Washington, and all three afterward general officers."

The writer enumerated many other distinguished Irishmen whom he had known in the army, and in social life ; among them Stephen Moylan, Major Butts, Colonel Keating, and Colonel Sharp Delaney. Mr. Biddle states also in this letter that most of the soldiers who, led by Wayne, stormed Stony Point, were Irish. This information greatly pleased the archbishop, who loved to hear that his countrymen had defended the land of their adoption. He loved that land most ardently ; yet he was broad and generous in his judgment and treatment of all nationalities. "In the annals of Church history," he once wrote, "there has never been a country which, in its civil and social relations, has exhibited so fair an opportunity for developing the practical harmonies of Catholic faith and of Catholic charity as the United States." He wished all foreigners to become naturalized as quickly as possible, and was opposed to the making of any distinction between native and foreign born Catholics.

In 1852 he renewed his attempt to organize a general debt-paying society for the benefit of the Churches of his diocese, and formed the "Auxiliary Church-building Association" for that purpose. But the society soon failed from lack of unity among the people. He could never get one congregation permanently to help another. Nevertheless, all the bankrupt Churches had been restored to a good financial condition, except St. Peter's in Barclay Street. This Church, lay-trustees had so mismanaged that its debt had increased from $116,500 in 1838, to $135,000 in 1844, when the corporation became bankrupt. One hundred thousand dollars of this debt was in notes given to poor people who had deposited their money with the trustees. The church was ordered to be sold; but the holders of these notes protested, and a scandalous five years' lawsuit was the result. The poor creditors appealed to the archbishop. In 1849 the Court of Appeals confirmed the assignment made by the trustees. The archbishop, however, tried to pay the notes, although he had no legal control of the property.

A layman was the assignee, and he was hostile to the archbishop who determined to expose the mismanagement of affairs, and for that purpose called a meeting of the chief parishioners, to be held in the basement of the church. When the assignee heard of this, he said to his friends, " The bishop is coming here this evening; I hope he will behave well. If he does, we shall treat him with respect; but if he does not, I shall say to him, ' Bishop, there is the door for you.' " But the archbishop gave such a scathing exposition of the mal-administration of the Church funds, that the assignee was obliged to leave the meeting, and the prelate's victory was complete. He acquired title to the whole property, and the trustees of St. Patrick's Church bought some lots on Fifth Avenue belonging to the embarrassed parish. These were the very lots on which St. Patrick's Cathedral now stands. A Church-Debt society was organized in St. Peter's parish. In a few years many of the notes were paid off, and the property saved. By law, the archbishop was authorized to pay the note-holders only sixty-five cents on the dollar; but he insisted on paying the full face-value of the notes to every one who presented them.

On Dec. 26, 1852, he caused a solemn Mass of thanksgiving to be sung in St. Peter's, on account of its liberation from financial embarrassment. He preached a sermon on the occasion, exposing, with great force, the evils and the scandals resulting from lay-trusteeism. A *Te Deum* was sung, and the whole Church rejoiced at the destruction of so baneful a system of Church administration.

In 1853 Monsignore Bedini, apostolic nuncio to the court of Brazil, passed through our country. He bore an autograph-letter from the Pope to the President of the United States, Franklin Pierce. The Monsignore was also to take counsel with the American bishops on several important matters affecting the interests of religion. He reached New York on June 30, and was the guest of the archbishop. They visited Washington, and saw the President, and then went to Milwaukee and to Montreal. The nuncio also consecrated the three new bishops, — Bishop Loughlin, of Brooklyn, who had been Vicar-General of New York; Bishop Bayley, of Newark, who had been Archbishop Hughes's secretary; and Bishop de Goesbriand, of Burlington, Vermont. About this time the archbishop consulted some members of the Cabinet at Washington about the appointment of a papal nuncio to the United States; but Mr. Campbell, the postmaster-general, wrote to him a letter which showed that the project was not looked on with favourable eyes: —

"In relation to the establishment of a nunciature to this country, the President will receive a *chargé*, or minister from the Pope; but he can only, of course, be received as his political representative. If his Holiness were to appoint a layman, there would be no difficulty in receiving him in the same manner as the representative of every other sovereign power is now received, charged, of course, only with the public affairs of the Pontifical States."

Many of the bishops of the country were pleased to hear that there would be no nuncio at Washington; for they feared that if one were appointed political influence might be attempted in appointments in the hierarchy in the United States.

The archbishop's health was again breaking down under his numerous labours, so he took a trip to Havana, thence to New Orleans, and returned to New York in May. During his absence some foreign radicals and refugees from European justice combined with native bigots to insult and to mob Monsignore Bedini in Cincinnati, Wheeling, and elsewhere. Even in New York, they threatened him, and watched the docks for his departure. The charge they brought against him was that he had been too severe in the administration of justice when he was papal legate at Bologna, where some revolutionists had been put to death during his administration. The mayor of our city advised him to go to Staten Island, and from that place of safety to board the steamer that was to take him to Europe. The nuncio followed the mayor's advice. When Archbishop Hughes returned from Cuba, and heard of this he was mortified and angered. He wrote at once to the nuncio:

"If I had been in New York, we should have taken a carriage at my door, even an open one if the day had been fine enough, and gone by the ordinary streets to the steamboat on which you were to embark. You will, perhaps, be astonished when I add, that in such an event, notwithstanding the lying clamours of the telegraph-wires and the newspapers, I do not believe that violence or insult would have been offered either to you, or to me, or to any one of our party."

Such was the archbishop's confidence in his own popularity and certainty of the fear which even the most desperate radicals had of his courage. Had a hair of his head been touched by the foreign revolutionists, their blood would have watered the spot where they dared to insult him. He was the idol of his flock, and specially beloved by the poor Irish of the city, who were proud of his ability, and loved him for his bravery. An apostate priest named Gavazzi was the chief instrument in circulating false stories about the nuncio. Gavazzi continued to create riots in many places in the country, even after the nuncio had left. He was a violent fanatic, and his intemperate language in abusing the Pope often provoked reprisals from some hotheaded Catholics who went to hear his harangues.

The archbishop's next controversy was with General Cass, United States Senator from Michigan. The Grand Duke of Tuscany, in virtue of the laws existing in his State, had imprisoned the family of the Madiai of Florence. The "Evangelical Alliance" circulated the report that this family was put in jail simply for "reading the Bible," and General Cass and others were so credulous as to believe the story. Bitter prejudice still existed in our country against the Catholic Church, and things were then believed at once which would now be carefully examined. The archbishop showed that the Madiai were imprisoned for public violations of law and disturbance of the public peace, and not for "reading the Bible." The next foe which the archbishop encountered was the New York "Times," which had asserted the existence of dissensions between the native and the foreign born bishops in the Church in the United States. Soon followed an attack on the archbishop, by John Mitchel, a leading member of the Young Ireland party. No one knows Mitchel's reason for this attack. It certainly did not promote the circulation of his newspaper, "The Citizen." The archbishop did not condescend to notice it, and the circulation of the paper diminished in consequence, and soon died. Mr. Mitchel, who was a gentleman of honour and culture, afterward regretted what he had done.

In 1854 a new eruption of the "Anti-Popery" mania took place; and a political party was formed, professing hostility to everything Catholic, and called by the name of the "Know-Nothings." They were the legitimate offspring of the "Native American" party of 1844. The principles of both parties were the same. Street-preachers from the heads of barrels began to abuse Catholics and denounce "Popery;" while even from the pulpit, ministers of the Gospel of peace preached violent sermons and urged violent measures against the Old Church. For a time New York, Louisville, and other cities seemed to become like Londonderry and Belfast in Ireland during the anniversary festivities of the Battle of the Boyne. Imported "Orangemen," who were not American citizens and who never intended to be, were prominent leaders in this "Know-Nothing" hostility to foreignism and to Catholicity. The archbishop, in this crisis, publicly, by writing and by speaking, warned his people to keep away from meetings in which their nationality or their religion was to be discussed, and ordered them to avoid the street-preachers who were tolerated and covertly supported by a "Know-Nothing" administration of the city. Some riots took place, and some Catholics were killed, but the "Know-Nothing," like the "Native American" party, being irrational and fundamentally Anti-American, died and was buried.

On the 30th of September, 1854, a provincial council was held in the archbishop's house. Seven bishops of the province, with the archbishop, were present. This was the first Provincial Council of New York. In its legislation, it followed the decrees of the Baltimore Councils. It made many laws for the enforcement of ecclesiastical discipline and the promotion of religious education. The archbishop established a regular chancery in his own diocese for the regulation of matrimonial dispensations, and appointed the Rev. Thomas S. Preston as chancellor. On the 18th of October the archbishop sailed for Europe, to be present at Rome at the proclamation of the dogma of the Immaculate Conception; that is, the declaration that the Blessed Mother of God was free from original sin at all times, even in the very first instant of the union of her soul and body. Bishop Timon, of Buffalo, and the Rev. Francis McNeirny, who afterward became Bishop of Albany, accompanied him on this voyage. They were in Rome on December 8, when his Holiness, Pius IX, surrounded by the cardinals and hundreds of bishops from all parts of the world, infallibly defined the doctrine that Mary, by a special privilege in view of her dignity as Mother of God, was preserved from the stain of original sin in which all ordinary mortals are conceived and born.

Before returning home, the archbishop visited England. He arrived in New York, March 27, 1855, and as usual began a controversy. This time it was with Erastus Brooks, State Senator from New York, and one of the editors of the "Express." Mr. Brooks was tainted with "Know-Nothing" prejudices. A bill was introduced into the State Legislature in the interest of the rebellious trustees of the Church of St. Louis, Buffalo, to take away from the bishops the right to hold Church property in their own name, and give this right entirely to trustees. If this bill had passed, the old trouble of the trustee system would have been revived. Mr. Brooks urged the passage of the bill, and in a speech in its favour told the Senate that he had found that John Hughes alone was the legal owner of five millions of dollars worth of real estate, in the city of New York. Mr. Brooks further said that transfers of real estate were made "not to John Hughes, Bishop, nor to John Hughes, Archbishop, nor to John Hughes, as trustee of the great Roman Catholic Church, but to plain John Hughes." The archbishop at once publicly declared that Mr. Brooks's statement was false. Brooks replied that there were fifty-eight entries of real estate transfers to the archbishop. An investigation, however, showed that there were only forty-six: several of these were duplicates; one or two were leases; one was a deed for a small bit of land two inches wide; one for the half of a burial-vault; and several related to property which was no longer held by the archbishop, but had been transferred by him to religious communities or to the trustees of the cathedral, or to others. Finally, it was shown that the actual deeds recorded in the archbishop's name were only thirty-three. This property, instead of being worth five millions, was worth only three hundred and eighty-five thousand dollars, and was mortgaged for two hundred and forty-five thousand dollars. The archbishop further showed that he derived no personal emolument from this property, and that he held it practically as trustee for the Church and for charitable purposes. In spite of the archbishop's protest, such was the power of the "Know-Nothing" vote, at the time, that the bill was passed by the legislature, but was never enforced, and in 1862 it was repealed.

The archbishop was again charged with being a politician and of intermeddling in politics. In the autumn of 1855 a report was circulated that he was using his influence to elect the candidate of the "Soft-Shell" democratic ticket. When he heard of this report he wrote "I have never been, and I never intend to be, a partisan in any political contest. I hold, and have ever held, that the position of a clergyman forbids him from taking any active part in such questions, and that he could not be a partisan without at once endangering and degrading his influence as a priest." Still, if the interest of religion required it, he knew how to use political influence, and he considered a priest always justified in interposing under such circumstances.

Cassius M. Clay, a well-known politician, wrote to him about this time concerning the "Catholic Vote."

Mr. Clay thought that the archbishop did or could control the political opinions and the political actions of his flock, and tried to prove that Catholics ought to be Republicans rather than Democrats. The archbishop replied : —

"I never influenced a human being, Catholic or Protestant, as to the party to which he might think proper to attach himself in his capacity as a voting citizen. I never voted but once in my life, and that vote was cast nearly thirty years ago in favour of your illustrious namesake and, I believe, relative, 'Harry of the West.' He was, in my estimation, a statesman as well as an orator, and I voted the more readily because my congregation were opposed to him, and some of them had almost threatened me on account of my good opinion of him, as a man much calumniated, but of whom, as a statesman and orator, his country might well be proud."

Few things in his life are more characteristic of the man than this voting for Henry Clay in opposition to the wishes and the threats of a whole congregation. He hated irrational prejudice in politics as well as in religion.

CHAPTER XII.

HIS HARD WORK FROM 1855 TO 1858. — HIS VISIT TO NEWFOUNDLAND. — ATTACKS ON HIS ADMINISTRATION OF THE DIOCESE. — HIS DEFENCE. — APOLOGIA PRO VITA SUA.

In September, 1855, the archbishop, invited by Bishop Mulloch, went to preach at the consecration of the new Catholic Cathedral in St. John's Newfoundland. He was received with extraordinary demonstrations of honour and affection; the whole Catholic population of the city, with the bishop at their head, turned out to receive him. Flags waved, bells were tolled, and cannon boomed when he landed; for he was beloved, admired, and honoured everywhere. He travelled much through the province, always working hard, preaching or officiating at some Church ceremony. On his return to New York, he praised the faith and the piety of the Newfoundland Catholics in an eloquent sermon preached in his own cathedral. His labours were incessant, visiting the Churches of the diocese, administering confirmation, settling disputes, and superintending the business affairs of all the parishes. In January, 1856, he lectured in Baltimore before the Young Catholic Friends' Society, on "The Present Condition and Prospects of the Catholic Church in the United States," and in June, of the same year, he lectured in Pittsburgh, on "The Relation between the Religious and Civil Duties of the Catholic Citizen."

He was overworked, and even his strong constitution could not stand the continual strain.

To recuperate, he tried exercise on horseback; but he soon tired of it. Then some of his friends bought him a country-house at Manhattanville, but he seldom visited it. It was therefore sold, and a new one bought on Madison Avenue and Thirty-Sixth Street, where he lived until his death. He made trips occasionally to the country or to the sea-shore; but he derived little benefit from them. He had injured his health by too much work, both physical and mental, and by irregularity in taking his meals. He sat up late to read or to study. He was often so interested in his mental work that he forgot the hour for dinner. He was afflicted with rheumatism and a complication of diseases the result of exposure and of excessive toil. Sometimes, however, the old fire flashed again. When he heard the bugle charge to combat, the old war-horse was ready for the fray. In December, 1856, disgusted with the unprincipled character of some Catholic newspapers, he published a noteworthy article in "The Metropolitan Record," a newspaper controlled by him, on "Reflections and Suggestions in Regard to What is called the Catholic Press in the United States." He attacked many of the Catholic papers. There were three classes of so-called journals which he considered injurious to the Church: first, those of the Young Ireland stamp, which were tainted with infidelity and radicalism; second, those which affected to consider the Church in the United States as an Irish or a German colony; and the third, those which tried to Americanize the Church, — that is, to minimize her doctrines and her discipline to suit national prejudices. Two prominent sympathizers with this last movement were Rev. Dr. Cummings, the first pastor of St. Stephen's Church, and Dr. Orestes A. Brownson, a convert from Protestantism, and the most distinguished review-writer of his time. Dr. Brownson, in an address to the graduates of St. John's College, in the early summer of 1856, spoke favourably of what was called the "Americanization" of the Church. The archbishop rose after the doctor was through, and publicly controverted his opinions. Some ill feeling between the archbishop and the "Americanizers" was the consequence. His article on the Press also displeased many. The ultra-Irish and the radical organs, as well as the "Liberals," attacked him. The Captain Dalgettys, the mercenaries of the Catholic Press of his day, would not listen to his advice. It was clearly and pointedly given. He wrote: —

"We advise that Catholic periodicals abstain from everything having a tendency to infringe on the regular ecclesiastical authority by which God has been pleased to appoint that his Church should be governed; that they shall not presume to draw odious comparisons, and publish them, between the clergy of one section of the country and those of another; that they shall not arrogate to themselves the position of oracles or umpires, to decide where is merit and where is demerit; that they shall not single out a clergyman for premature panegyric simply because he is a patron of this or that journal, while they pass over in silence other clergymen oftentimes of more than equal worth."

His words went home and hurt the guilty. His hot shot provoked a reply. One of the malcontents attacked him in the New York "Times," in January, 1857, under the signature of "Equitas." The editor of the "Times," Mr. Henry J. Raymond, published the letter of "Equitas," supposing it to be the genuine production of a venerable Boston priest, whose name was forged and appended to it. While Mr. Raymond was in Europe, the same "Equitas" published in the "Times" another attack more violent than the first, charging the archbishop with "maladministration, nepotism, indolence, arrogance, and a meddling and petty spirit;" "of indifference to the Virgin Mary," for having omitted to notice with due solemnities "the declaration of the dogma of the Immaculate Conception;" and of "disrespect to the representative of the Vicar of Christ on earth," because the archbishop "turned his back and fled to Cuba, when the nuncio of Pius IX., assailed by the Press, hooted and stoned by the mob, and burned in effigy in a hundred cities and villages, most needed his support."

The archbishop was sensitive and jealous of his good name at home and abroad, but particularly at Rome. He felt keenly, therefore, this brutal attack on his character as a loyal Catholic and an archbishop. His malicious and cowardly anonymous assailant sent the articles signed "Equitas" to many bishops and even to cardinals in Rome; and he feared that some of them would believe the statements made against his character and his administration. He therefore answered the charges of "Equitas" in detail, and took care that his friends and his enemies should read his replies. Speaking of his conduct toward his flock he writes: —

"The circumstances by which I have been surrounded, and the character of the country and people with whom I had to deal, did not allow me to use, at all times, that meek and apostolic spirit which is so appropriate and beautiful, and for which Roman writers are so specially distinguished. The people of this country, and especially those among whom I have lived, have great respect for a manly, straight-forward, and outspoken vindication of any rights, whether civil or ecclesiastical, which men deem worthy to be defended at all. . . . I had to stand up among these people as their bishop and chief; to warn them against the dangers that surrounded them; to contend for their rights as a religious community; to repel the spirit of faction among them; to convince their judgment by frequent explanations in regard to public and mixed questions; to encourage the timid; and sometimes to restrain the impetuous, — in short, to knead them up into one dough, to be leavened by the spirit of Catholic faith and of Catholic union."

The document in which these words are found, was really an *Apologia pro vita sua*. He sent it to Rome, and Cardinal Barnabo, the prefect of the Propaganda, was so pleased, after reading it, that he sent the archbishop a message of love and of congratulation. The cardinal expressed admiration for the penetrating mind of the Archbishop of New York, "in judging not only the past, but also the future of the American Church."

In the spring of 1857 a priest from the Western States, named Tracy, came to New York in the interest of parties who wished to establish an Irish colony in Nebraska, by getting emigrants from the Eastern cities. Father Tracy had much influential support among the clergy of our large cities, who thought that it would be a blessing if the Irish poor could be induced to leave the cities and villages and to settle on farms in the West. And so it would have been, if the attempt to remove the poor from the congested centres in the East had been financially backed and properly managed. A meeting was held to further the scheme in the old Broadway Tabernacle. Many prominent laymen and well-known priests attended it. Father Tracy addressed the audience, but in the midst of his speech he was interrupted by the archbishop, who had gone to the gallery in disguise. He showed the absurdity of the projected undertaking as there was no financier behind it. He catechised Father Tracy, and finally denounced the whole affair. The archbishop was right. The few Irishmen who went from New York, induced by the promises held out to them, soon came back penniless and heart-broken.

The progress of the Catholic Church in this State, and the continual labours of the archbishop, may be judged from a letter which he wrote, May 26, 1858, to his friend Bishop McNally, of Clogher in Ireland. This was just after the dedication, in East Fourteenth Street, of the new Catholic church under the title of the "Immaculate Conception." "You will be, perhaps, surprised," writes his Grace, "when I mention that this is the ninety-ninth church that has been erected and dedicated under my personal guidance and responsibility since the period of my appointment as Bishop of New York; and from this simple fact you will easily infer that what remains of mind and body to one who has gone through so much, must be henceforward of little advantage to the Church or the people committed to my care."

After such a record of labour, no wonder fatigue oppressed him. He often entertained the idea of resigning his office. He longed for the leisure, not found in an active life, to read and to study. He even expressed a wish to this effect to the Roman authorities. But Cardinal Barnabo, the prefect of the Propaganda, who esteemed and loved him, would not hear of a resignation. The archbishop then asked for a coadjutor; this clearly showed that he had broken down. It was only a few years before that he had said to a friend, "They may do what they like with the diocese when I am under the ground, but so long as I live there shall be no coadjutor bishop of New York." He now consulted his suffragans, and told them his wishes, and even named his choice for the coadjutorship; but they begged him to delay. They were afraid that he would resign after getting a coadjutor; for he was very feeble, and began to retire more and more from the public gaze. He sought seclusion, and seemed to decline any longer to enter into conflict. The establishment of the North American College at Rome, however, for a time roused his energies. Pius IX. proposed, in a letter to the bishops of the United States in 1855, to found this college, and in 1857 bought for that purpose the old convent of the Visitation nuns, the Umiltà, in the street of that name at Rome. The Pope paid forty-two thousand *Scudi* for it, and gave the use of it to the American bishops. The bishops were to furnish only the running expenses. The pupils were to attend the Propaganda course of studies. The rector was to be selected by his Holiness, from three candidates nominated by the bishops of the United States. The archbishop took the deepest interest in the enterprise ; and when the college was opened, Dec. 8, 1858, it contained many students from New York, and from the suffragan dioceses. One of the first students was Michael A. Corrigan, then of Newark, New Jersey, now Archbishop of New York.

The building of the new cathedral in Fiftieth Street also occupied his Grace's attention. He laid the corner stone of it on August 15, 1858, in the presence of seven bishops, one hundred and thirty priests, and over one hundred thousand people. About this time the Atlantic cable was laid between Europe and America. The archbishop was invited to the ceremonies at the completion of this great work. He made one of the addresses on the occasion, and was present at the banquet which followed. He continued the work on the cathedral until August, 1860, when the walls were twelve or fourteen feet high, and then stopped building for lack of funds, and because civil war had broken out and disturbed the finances of the country. Cardinel McCloskey completed the work, except the towers and some altars, which have since been erected by Archbishop Corrigan.

In 1859 and 1860 "The Roman Question" became unusually interesting. The Sardinian king and his ministers were plotting the destruction of the Pope's temporal sovereignty, and using every means to accomplish their purpose. The chiefs of the Italian secret societies were in their pay, and while preaching a republic, were really working to make the dynasty of Savoy the ruler of all Italy. The plot was to destroy the grand duchies of North Italy, expel the Bourbon dynasty from Naples and Sicily, steal the Pope's territory, and make a united Italy under King Victor Emmanuel. His prime minister Cavour was the arch plotter; but the Emperor of France, Napoleon III., and the ambitious Bismarck, then prime minister of the King of Prussia, were in collusion with the Italian statesman. The secret societies, particularly the Carbonari, and that reckless soldier of fortune Garibaldi, were only pawns on the Italian chess-board at which Cavour sat and played. But it was difficult to destroy the papal temporal sovereignty, for it was guaranteed by treaties, and had been protected by a French army of occupation since 1848. Against this sovereignty, all arms were employed, and all means used. Diplomacy, conspiracy, deception, slander, and finally fraud and violence were Cavour's weapons. Writers in France, and throughout the whole of Europe, wrote to show that the temporal power of the Pope should be destroyed, and the Italian treasury was depleted in the propaganda of Sardinian ambition and Mazzinian plotting. A war of pamphlets was waged in Europe on this theme. The Archbishop of New York, in spite of his many physical infirmities, at once took a hand in the fray. He wrote a pastoral letter in reply to the European attacks on the temporal power of the Pope, showing its necessity as a guarantee of the spiritual independence of the Church. The Pope can be no king's subject, argued the archbishop, because he is the head, not of a national, but of a universal Church. The Pope as a subject of the King of Italy may be impeded by the civil laws from the exercise of his duties as head of the Church, even in Italy; his intercourse with the rest of the Catholic world may also be impeded, and the Church may have no means of knowing whether papal documents or decisions are genuine or not, since they may be stopped at the national frontier or forged in an Italian post-office. In case of war between Italy and France, for instance, how can French Catholics have free access to the

Holy See How could the French bishops without being accused of treasonable practices, have free intercourse with the head of their Church, if he be an Italian subject ? Just as in our republic there is a small district set apart for the central government of the country, — a district distinct and independent of the States, — so in the Church should there be a small sovereignty under the exclusive control of the Church, to guarantee the freedom of her executive, and prevent its being controlled by any nation. This was the archbishop's line of argument. The Pope and the cardinals were pleased with his pastoral, and caused it to be translated into Italian and to be published by the Propaganda Press at Rome.

In 1860, suffering from a complication of disorders, he made a trip to the South, accompanied by his chaplain. At Charleston, he met Bishop Lynch of that see, and together they travelled to St. Augustine, Florida. After an absence of four weeks he returned, much improved in health. But he was attacked by Bright's disease of the kidneys, the malady of which he died. On April 4, 1860, he wrote a letter to the distinguished lawyer Charles O'Conor, on the question of the Pope's temporal sovereignty. In this letter the archbishop says : —

"The main thing is that the spiritual father of more than two hundred millions of Catholics all over the globe, shall not be a subject of the King of Sardinia, or of the

Emperor of France, or of any other king on the globe. Private individuals may enjoy freedom in a moderate sense under any sovereign or even despot. But not so the Pope. We want the Vicar of Christ to be free; and this implies that there must be some portion of the earth of which he shall be the recognized sovereign. God knows it might be better to exercise the plentitude of power without any care of state; but as the world is constituted, this is impossible."

It was proposed to hold a public meeting to express sympathy with the Holy See in its conflict with the revolutionists and radicals, and to insist on its right to temporal power. But some prominent laymen, and finally the archbishop, thought it wiser to give pecuniary aid to the Roman authorities, rather than mere expressions of sympathy. Accordingly, the archbishop ordered collections to be taken up in all the Churches, and sent the amount to his Holiness, with an address signed by the clergy and by the chief Catholic laymen of the city. On June 24 he preached in the cathedral a well-prepared sermon on the temporal power of the Holy See. He took strong ground against the Sardinian intriguers, and argued that the Pope, as an independent sovereign, should be allowed to govern his own States in his own way. The sermon was attacked by many of the secular and sectarian papers, and the archbishop replied to his critics in the "Metropolitan Record." The papal collection realized on this occasion the very large amount of fifty-three thousand dollars. This sermon was one of the best composed ever delivered by the archbishop. His oratory was always forcible and impressive, particularly in his younger days. He had a fine voice and a distinguished presence.

A correspondent for a Southern newspaper, who had heard him preach, thus describes the archbishop's style of preaching in his old age: —

"One saw in the preacher an elderly man in infirm health, of bowed form, yet of striking appearance. He wore a tight-fitting cassock, ornamented with a row of red buttons down the front and down the sleeves, and surmounted by a doctor's cape. On his breast there lay a graven cross of gold, suspended by a heavy golden chain, and on his finger appeared the episcopal ring, which flashed strange light into the wondering eyes of poor Protestants. The style of the preacher, and the service for devotion, were simple even unto plainness. He and Father McNeirny pulled aside the desk which held King James's Bible (it was the Douay Catholic Bible, not King James's), so that no screen separated him from his audience. From the reply of our Saviour to the question of the tempting lawyers, as it is recorded in the 22d chapter of St. Matthew, he discoursed on love to God and love to man, and the densely packed audience listened with scarcely a stir for an hour and three quarters."

But the voice that could sway multitudes was growing weak and was soon to be stilled in death.

CHAPTER XIII.

Archbishop Hughes as a Poet.

The archbishop's letters and controversial writings are so well known and so numerous, that a criticism on them would require a volume of its own. He knew little of the literature of the modern foreign languages, except at second-hand. He was not a linguist; he never had the leisure nor the opportunity, even if he had the inclination, to devote himself to literature for its own sake. Whatever of it he studied, however, he knew well. He read the best English writers and modeled his style after them; consequently it is not disfigured by foreign idioms or phrases. He always wrote clear, straightforward, and pungent English; and some of his works are well worthy of imitation by all who aim at the acquisition of force and precision in the expression of thought.

The whole world knows him as a polemic of the first class; but not so many know him as a poet. Yet in his early days he cultivated the muses, and has left us a few poems which show an excellent imagination and a facility for making good verses. Had he continued to write verses, they might have attained the excellence of his prose. The reader will perhaps thank us for giving him a chance to read a few of these poems. We quote also a poetical description of a storm at sea, written by him after he became a bishop. It will show a phase in his character not publicly known; that he who was so fierce in his invective, so biting in his sarcasm, and so inexorable in his logic when dealing with an adversary, could be tranquil and gentle when he wished, and paint a picture from Nature with grace, elegance, and grandeur.

TO THE HOME OF MY FATHERS.

Does Freedom yet breathe in the bard's rustic number?
   Can his harp, by the genius of liberty strung,
Be mute, while the land where his forefathers slumber
   Is bleeding in bondage, and bleeding unsung?

. . . .

Is no Washington near thee, thou captive of ages,
   To marshal thy brave ones and lead them to war?
Is no Franklin arrayed in the list of thy sages?
   In that of thy heroes, no young Bolivar?

Thy sons must forsake thee, if worth bids them cherish
   A hope on the records of glory to shine.
Does not Wellington reign? Had not Emmet to perish?
   The laurel is England's; the cypress is thine.

But weep not, poor Erin, though Emmet is wanting;
  His spirit still lives in the hearts of the brave.
There are bosoms behind, as devotedly panting
  For the breath of the free or the boon of the grave.

And Hope tells my heart that a day will be given,
  When the chain shall be loosed and their sorrows redressed;
When thou shalt go forth in the pride of thy even,
  As free as the zephyrs that sport on thy breast.

Oh, then shall thy harp, which has slumbered in sadness,
  Feel the pulse of fair Freedom that erst made it thrill;
Then the bard shall awake it in accents of gladness,
  And sweep its wild chords on thy ever-green hill.

And, oh, when the last scene of Nature is closing,
  When this spirit of mine shall burst forth and be free,
How calm could I rest, on thy bosom reposing,
  Thou home of my fathers! Green Isle of the sea!

Although this poem shows his intense love for his native land, yet it is a fact that he was not clannishly Irish. The priests and the people of other nationalities were happy under his just and equable sway.

The following poem written to a friend shows how little in youth he anticipated his future career: —

And, ah, when the minstrel, too proud or too humble
  To sue for a place on the legends of fame,
Shall sleep in the tomb, like his fathers to crumble,
  Divulge not, Æmilius, divulge not his name.

But if in the twilight perchance thou shouldst wander
To where he shall slumber, unhonoured, unknown,
Be the dirge thou wilt sing o'er the grave of Leander,
"Here resteth a heart which was part of my own!"

ODE TO DEATH.

King conquers king, and slave his fellow-slave;
    But slave and king shall fall
    In thy sepulchral hall,
Whilst thou grim monarch, shalt triumphant wave
Thy iron sceptre o'er their equal grave,
    Dread conqueror of all!

Those fools who fight for lords and thrones,
    To thee at length shall yield
    The helmet, lance, and shield,
When princely pride shall ask their dying groans,
Or wish the tribute of their valiant bones,
    To whiten on a field.

. . . .

Yet be not proud in thy resistless sway,
    Thou scourge of human crime
    In every land and clime;
For on the confines of eternal day
Thou too shalt fall, an angel's easy prey,
    Upon the tomb of Time.

How he detested American slavery is shown in the following poem:—

THE SLAVE.

Hard is the lot of him who's doomed to toil,
Without one slender hope to soothe his pain,
Whose sweat and labour are a master's spoil,
Whose sad reward a master's proud disdain.
Wipe from thy code, Columbia, wipe the stain;
Be free as air, but yet be kind as free,
And chase foul bondage from thy Southern plain.
If such the right of man, by heaven's decree,
Oh, then let Afric's sons feel what it is — to be.

. . . .

In hot meridian day, of late, I hied
To court the covert of a spreading oak;
I sat beneath, and thence, in pity, eyed
The negro moiling at his daily yoke.
And still he plied the dull, desponding stroke
Beneath the scorching of the noon-tide sun,
Sullen and silent; or if words he spoke,
I could not hear; but ever and anon
I heard the lash which even brutes are fain to shun.

The ruthless driver soon was forced to yield:
Though strong of sinew, still he could not bear
The tyrant labours of the parching field,
But sought the shade to breathe a cooler air;
Whilst, less inhuman, but, alas! less fair,
The drudging slave began to pour his song
Upon the heedless wind, and breathe despair.
He sung the negroes' foul, unpitied wrong,
Sad and ironical — late he felt the thong.

"Hail Columbia, happy land!
　Where Freedom waves her golden wand,
　　Where equal justice reigns.
　But, ah, Columbia, great and free,
　Has not a boon for mine and me,
　　But slavery and chains.
　Oh, once I had a soothing Joy,
　　The hope of other years,
　That free Columbia would destroy
　　The source of these my tears.
　　But pining, declining,
　　I still drag to the grave,
　　Doomed to sigh till I die,
　　Free Columbia's slave.

"Hail Columbia, happy land!
　Whose sons, a free, a heaven-born band,
　　Will free us soon with blows, —
　If freeman's freest blood were shed,
　Could it be purer or more red
　　Than this of mine that flows?
　'T was freeman's whip that brought this gore
　　That trickles down my breast;
　But soon my bleeding will be o'er,
　　My grave will yield me rest.
　　I will then, until then,
　　Abide my hard and hopeless lot;
　　But there's room in the tomb
　　For freemen too to rot.

"Hail Columbia, happy land!
　Where those who show a fairer hand

> Enjoy sweet liberty.
> But from the moment of my birth
> I slave along Columbia's earth;
> Nor Freedom smiles on me.
> Long have I pined through years of woe
> Adown life's bleeding track,
> And still my tears, my blood must flow,
> Because my hand is black.
> Still boiling, still toiling,
> Beneath the burning heats of noon,
> I, poor slave, court the grave;
> O Columbia, grant the boon!
>
> "Hail Columbia hap —"
>
> He ceased the song, and heaved another sigh
> In silent, cheerless mood; for, ah, the while
> The driver's hated steps were drawing nigh,
> Nor song of woe, nor words dare then beguile
> The goaded sorrows of a thing so vile.
> Yet such the plaintive song that caught my ear,
> That cold humanity may blush to smile,
> When dove-eyed Mercy softly leans to hear,
> And Pity turns aside to shed another tear.

Certainly no poet of the "Native American" or old "Know-Nothing" party could sing more loyally than he does of the land he loved, and for whose liberty and union he spent the last years of his life in toil.

JUBILEE OF AMERICAN FREEDOM.

Great Lord of creation, we owe it to thee,
That our country is kingless, our people are free!
Oh, grant a like boon to that ill-fated Isle
Where the ruled are as brave as their rulers are vile;
Where genius illumines, and minds are sincere;
Where hearts beat in bosoms that never felt fear.
Yes, children of freemen, your fathers could tell
How the Irishman fought, till he conquered or fell;
How the hero stood still when the heartless were flying;
How Arnold betrayed while Montgomery was dying!
Poor Erin, thy sons shall have fame in our story;
Their sickles were mixed in our harvest of glory.
Columbia invites thee to rise and be free,
Till she call thee her sister, thou gem of the sea.
But, hark! Oh, that song swelling higher and higher!
'T is the voice of Columbia, attuned to the lyre;
'T is her thankgiving anthem, and millions combine
In the chorus of love around Liberty's shrine.

" Peace to the patriot, setting in glory;
His eye hath grown dim, and his locks have grown hoary.
He balanced no sceptre, he cushioned no throne;
He was wise for his country, his country alone.

" Peace to the ashes of heroes that sleep
In the battle-field grave, or the cells of the deep;
Their deeds be the theme of both story and art,
But their names are inscribed in the book of my heart.

"The holy inheritance their blood hath won
Shall descend in succession from father to son
Till the trumpet-tongued angel check Time in his flight,
And the dawn of eternity burst on my sight.

"Peace to my sons, and my rosy-crowned daughters,
My mountains, my oceans, my cities, my waters!
And peace to the stranger whom tyrants oppressed;
Let him come to my bosom and slumber at rest.

CHORUS.

"It is Liberty's jubilee, swell the loud chorus!
Half an age hath gone by,—there are whole ones before
    us;
That iron chain, rent by our fathers of old,
Is not fit for sons, though its links were of gold."

The following is really a prose poem, written at sea. It shows how much he loved Nature, and how well he could describe her: —

"On the 31st I was gratified with a spectacle which I had often desired to witness,—the condition of the sea during a tempest. . . . After a breeze from the north and northwest of about sixty hours' continuance, the wind died away about four o'clock. The calm continued until about nine o'clock in the evening, as if the wind had ceased to blow, excepting a few puffs that were floating about, bewildered, and not knowing what to do with themselves. In the interval the mercury in the barometer had fallen at an extraordinary rate, and the captain predicted that we were likely to encounter 'a gale' from the south-east. I did not hear the remark at the time, or I should not probably have gone to bed. The gale came on, however, at about eleven o'clock, — not violent at first but increasing every moment. I slept soundly, as usual, until half-past five in the morning, although I had a confused and dreamy recollection of a good deal of rolling and thumping during the night, occasioned by the unsteady course of the ship and the dashing of the waves.

"On the deck, most of the passengers had by this time congregated. I found them clinging to whatever they could hold on by around the doors of the hurricane house, and looking on in silence and consternation. 'Ha! ha!' I said to myself, 'this is what I have been wanting, but *c' est un peu trop.*' It was still quite dark. Four of the principal sails were already in ribbons. The winds were howling through the cordage, the rain dashing along furiously and in torrents, while the noise and whirl-gusts of spray reminded one of the scene behind the great cataract of Niagara. In the midst of all this were the captain with his speaking-trumpet, the officers and sailors screaming out to each other in their efforts to be heard, and, incredible as it may seem and should be, swelling the gale with their oaths and curses. All this, taken together, in the darkness, or rather twilight, of the hour, and the fury of the hurricane, combined as much of the terribly sublime as I ever wish to witness concentrated in one scene. This was but the commencement of the gale, which, however, had taken us by surprise, and borrowed additional terrors from the darkness and suddenness with which it came upon us. It lasted twenty-four hours, so that through the whole of that day I had an opportunity of enjoying at leisure, a scene which, apart from the danger, would be at any time worth a voyage across the Atlantic.

The hurricane did not acquire its full force until about nine o'clock. By that time there was no more work to be done. The vessel "lay to," as they term it, and those who had charge of her stood by only to see and meet whatever disaster might occur. It was now breakfast-time, but cooking had been out of the question and appetite was nearly so. My own was excellent, — especially for the small allowance of a fast day. By this time the sea had put on its hurricane billows, and not to lose the opportunity, after having fortified myself with appropriate clothing, I took my position on a part of the quarter-deck from which I could survey the whole scene around the ship undisturbed, and with entire safety to myself so long as her strong works should hold together. I had often seen and admired paintings of a storm at sea, and my recollections of them enabled me to compare them with the original, by which I was now surrounded. Those paintings, in general, are true so far as they go; but after all, how feeble is the representation, and how destitute of those accompaniments which art cannot supply! In the painting you have, it is true, the ship and the sea agitated by the storm, but motion — the very life and spirit of the subject — is lost in the imitation; it is arrested, and the whole becomes stationary as the canvas itself. Imagination, indeed, comes to the painter's aid in this perhaps more than any other subject of the mere physical order. But not for the eye alone has the sea-storm the many parts by whose wild harmony it becomes at once beautiful, terrible, and sublime. For even could the pencil be successful in representing it so far as the eye is concerned, there would still be wanting the rushing of the tempest, the groaning of the spars and masts, the quick, shrill whistling of the cordage and rigging, and more than all, the ponderous dashing of the uplifted deep. . . . The weather was thick and hazy, more especially along the surface of the sea. It was impossible to see more than three-quarters of a mile in any direction; but within this contracted horizon you saw the mountain waves rising suddenly out of the darkness on one side, and rushing and tumbling across the valleys that remained from the passage of their predecessors, until, like them, they rolled away into darkness on the other side. These waves were not either numerous or rapid in their course, but their massiveness and elevation were such as it seems a tempest alone has power to produce. It must have been the refraction of light falling on their sides that gave to these waves, especially near their summit, the most beautiful, clear, green colour, as if they were composed of irregular and disturbed heaps of molten and transparent, emerald-crowned water with a topping of white foam, which, as the wave approached, would spill itself over on the side nearest you and come tumbling down with the dash of a cataract. Not less magnificent than the waves themselves were the valleys of different and varying dimensions that remained between them; their waters had lost for a moment the onward motion of the billows, but they were far from being at rest. Under their scarf of foam they preserved the same green colour of the mighty insurgents that had passed over them. But the symptoms of violence which had been presented to the eye, boiling and wheeling about rapidly in currents and eddies, with the surface glowing and hissing as if it had come in contact with red-hot iron, all showed that even these low places were not unvisited by the storm, but that its angry spirit had descended into its depths, ready to heave them up into all the rushing violence of the general commotion. It was impossible not to be impressed with a deep feeling of awe at the universal majesty of that God who has created and preserves all this wondrous combination of the elements. The Scriptures speak of him, in the midst of thunder and lightning, as riding in the whirlwind and walking on the deep, and at such a moment how could I forget His presence who alone unbinds or restrains the fury of winds and waves at his pleasure? Here they were raging with indescribable fierceness, and yet man, of such limited strength as to his physical structure, was now in the act of triumphing over their fierceness. By using his reason, — that feeble ray of the divine intelligence which has been imparted to him, — he builds his house on the foundation of the waters and the tempest cannot overturn it. . . .

CHAPTER XIV.

HIS PATRIOTISM. — HIS ASSISTANCE TO THE GOVERNMENT DURING OUR CIVIL WAR. — HIS MISSION TO EUROPE TO HELP THE CAUSE OF THE UNITED STATES. — INTERVIEW WITH NAPOLEON III. — RETURN TO NEW YORK. — HIS LAST SERMON. — THE DRAFT-RIOTS. — HIS SPEECH TO THE MOB. — HIS LAST SICKNESS AND DEATH.

ARCHBISHOP HUGHES, like other great Irish Catholics such as Daniel O'Connell and the Rev. Father Matthew, the apostle of temperance, was a foe of negro slavery, and of slavery of every description. He had suffered from slavery at home, and therefore sympathized with all who were oppressed. In his early days, when he had cultivated a taste for poetry, he wrote the verses in which he urged Columbia "to chase foul bondage from her Southern plain." He also expressed himself as opposed to the institution of slavery, in his controversy with Dr. Breckinridge; but the archbishop was not an Abolitionist. He was opposed to Northern interference with the domestic institutions of the South. When, therefore,

Daniel O'Connell, Father Matthew, and other prominent Anti-slavery Irishmen published an address which the Abolitionists tried to use for their illegal purposes, the archbishop, explaining his views, wrote a letter to the "Courier and Enquirer," in March, 1842. He says in it: "I am no friend to slavery, but I am still less friendly to any attempt of foreign origin to abolish it." He believed in the Monroe doctrine, that no foreigners should be allowed to interfere in American affairs; and that if foreigners came to live here, they should become loyal citizens of the republic and give up their allegiance to foreign potentates. After seeing and studying the condition of the negro slaves in Cuba and in our Southern States, his views became quite moderate, and he feared and opposed all plans which aimed at the sudden emancipation of a people unprepared for liberty. He thought that a violent or an unprepared emancipation would be injurious to the negroes both physically and morally. In this he disagreed with the distinguished convert, Dr. Orestes Brownson, who openly advocated their immediate emancipation. Then some enemies went so far as to accuse the archbishop of being in favour of the slave-trade. This calumny was often repeated, and was published in some of the French newspapers, in 1861 and 1862, when he was in Paris. He there took occasion to deny the charge, stating that although he was opposed to Abolitionism, he was not, "never had been, and never could be an advocate of slavery." He advocated the abolition of slavery in each State by its own local and legal authority, and not by Congress. In a letter to Bishop Lynch, of Charleston, in August, 1861, we find these words: —

"I am an advocate for the sovereignty of every State in the Union within the limits recognized and approved by its own representative authority when the constitution was agreed on. As a consequence, I hold that South Carolina has no State right to interfere with the internal affairs of Massachusetts; and as a further consequence, that Massachusetts has no right to interfere with South Carolina in its domestic and civil affairs, as one of the sovereign States of this now threatened Union."

He was a strong Union man, and zealously opposed the rebellion of the South. He wrote in May, 1861, to a Southern bishop, —

"The South has taken upon itself to be judge in its own cause, to be witness in its own cause, and to execute, if necessary, by force of arms its own decision. In a constitutional country this means either revolution or rebellion, since there are tribunals agreed upon by North and South, and supported by both for a period of more than seventy years. When these tribunals are set aside, and men appeal to the sword, the Federal Government has only to abdicate, or meet sword with sword."

The archbishop never changed these views. When the central Government was engaged in war for the restoration of the Union, and after President Lincoln's emancipation proclamation, the archbishop boldly declared himself in favour of the strongest measures for the support of the Federal authority. He gave every help that he could to the Government, and it was very great, for he was regarded as the leader of all the Catholics in the country. He corresponded frequently with his old friend Mr. Seward, the Secretary of State, and showed the foresight of the statesman as well as the ability of a great military leader in this correspondence. He saw the necessity of keeping a large army between Richmond and Washington, and pointed out the strategic importance of Cairo on the Mississippi. He studied the geography and the strategic points of the country like a military man, and became intensely interested in the struggle and in the movement of the troops. He urged on Mr. Seward, even as early in the war as April, 1861, the necessity of keeping an army of at least one hundred thousand men about Washington. He thought it better to incur great expense at once, "in order to save greater expense in the feeble drag of a contest wherein the forces are entirely or nearly balanced." He wrote:—

"Let the question of the rights of the Federal Government over the whole country be settled once and forever. Let there be no compromise until the States shall be disposed to return to their allegiance to the Federal Government, which they themselves contributed to create, and from which nothing new in the legislation of the Federal Government has given them the slightest pretext for seceding; let there be no recognition of the pretended government of the Confederate States, no negotiation with them as such, but ample kindness toward the States taken one by one."

He declared the rebel privateers "essentially pirates;" and that the American cruisers ought to sink them as pirates. Again he writes to Mr. Seward: "Old Cato used to say 'delenda est Carthago!'[1] I would say, 'Augenda est Cairo!'"[2] He wanted Cairo well protected and fortified so as to control the Mississippi River. Yet he advised mildness and kindness wherever possible. Still writing to Mr. Seward, he said: —

"There is only one word I would add; and that is, that in your effort to bring back the Southern States to their condition before the war, you would, as far as it would be consistent with the high principle of supreme government, be as patient and as considerate toward the State authorities of this so-called confederacy as possible. Conquest is not altogether by the sword. Statesmanship, and especially in our circumstances, may have much to do with it. But no backing down of the Federal Government. . . . I am getting old, and it is time for me to begin to gather myself up for a transition from this world to another, and as I hope a better. I know that this world

---

[1] Carthage must be destroyed.
[2] Cairo must be strengthened.

would have gone on well, just as well as it has done, had I never lived. At the same time, as I mentioned in my first letter, I have not been able to sever my thoughts and my feelings from what has occurred almost under my eyes, in the only country which I call mine, and to which I am devoted by every prompting of my understanding, and by every loyal sentiment of my heart."

In this note how strongly marked is the patriotism of the great archbishop! Who could love his country more than he? That love was in the very core of his heart.

Mr. Seward, to whom these letters were written, answered that he had shown them to President Lincoln, who was so well pleased with the last one that he caused a copy of it to be made for his own special use. The President had already written to him on Oct. 21, 1861, asking his aid in the appointment of Catholic chaplains for the army hospitals. President Lincoln had the most profound respect for his ability and for his holy office.

In October, 1861, he was invited by Mr. Seward to go to Washington for a private conference. Messrs. Mason and Slidell had a short time before gone to Europe as Commissioners from the Southern Confederacy, to influence, if possible, England and France in its favour. To counteract their efforts, the United States Government asked Archbishop Hughes to go to France, and Mr. Thurlow Weed to go to England.

Both sailed together from New York on November 6. The archbishop was also accompanied by his private secretary, the Rev. Francis McNeirny. When they arrived in Paris, his Grace called on the American minister, Mr. Dayton, and then wrote to Mr. Seward from the *Hotel de l'Empire:* " Mr. Dayton is the representative of our Government. So am I; but in a different order. For I would have been its representative under any possible circumstances so far as concerns a right to think and speak in behalf of the only nation on the face of the earth to which I owe allegiance and loyalty." The archbishop's letters to Mr. Seward showed great diplomatic talent. He had interviews in Paris with M. Thouvenel, the French minister of foreign affairs, and finally with the emperor and the empress of the French. He tried to impress on his hearers the futility of the Southern attempt to break up the United States. He pointed out the strength of the Union cause and the folly of any foreign government attempting to support the Southern Rebellion.

He had a long interview with Napoleon III. and the empress, whom he tried to disabuse of their prejudices against the North. Said the empress toward the close of this interview: —

" How can this blockade be sustained along so extensive a coast? It cannot last. Napoleon I. had that topic in his mind during the war with England;

and with all his immense capacity he gave it up as impracticable."

The archbishop replied: —

"Imperial lady, if Napoleon I. had been acquainted, for maritime purposes, with the power of steam and the velocity of electric communication by telegraph, his dynasty would not have suffered an interruption; and where England would be at this day under such circumstances it would be hazardous to say."

His interview with their Majesties was long and cordial; and his words produced a profound impression.

From Paris, in January, 1862, he wrote to Secretary Seward, urging the necessity of coast defences and fortifications in the United States. His love of the country of his adoption had complete possession of his soul. He left Paris in February of the same year and visited Ireland, defending the United States Government wherever he travelled, and winning sympathy for the North in her struggle against rebellion. His presence in the Green Isle was hailed with enthusiasm. The personal attachment of the Irish for him, he used for the benefit of the United States. He had much to do with creating the general sympathy of the Irish in Ireland for the Union cause; and the knowledge of this sympathy prevented England from taking sides with the Southern Confederacy. The archbishop wrote to Mr. Seward that the English Government could not recruit an army in Ireland to fight against the United States; the people of Ireland hated England too much on their own account to co-operate with any attempt to destroy the American republic which they loved.

Later in February he went to Rome, and there again at the centre of Christianity, used all his influence to create sentiments favourable to the Union cause. His letters to Mr. Seward give an account of his travels and interviews with prominent people, and tell of his efforts to convert those who favoured the rebels. He saw the Pope, and pointed out the error and the wrong of the rebellion. On February 21 he writes to Mr. Seward: "The Holy Father has been particularly kind. He and Antonelli[1] both speak of you with kind remembrance and with great respect." Of President Lincoln he writes: "There has been no president of the United States more capable, more honest, more moderate, more safe and reliable than the actual incumbent who is at the head of the country."

The archbishop lodged at the American College during his stay at Rome. He became so ill that it was feared he would die; still again and again he rallied. The city contained a large number of strangers who had come to witness the ceremony of the canonization of the Japanese martyrs, put to death in the time of Saint Francis Xavier for profess-

---

[1] The great secretary of state of Pius IX.

ing the Christian faith. This ceremony took place in June, 1862. The archbishop was a conspicuous figure among the prelates present. Distinguished people from all over the world called to pay their respects to him. Some of the Southern Catholics were, however, bitterly hostile to him, and complained that his influence had prevented England and France from recognizing the Southern Confederacy. Although very infirm, he took part in many Church ceremonies, and once officiated at the devotion of the "Stations of the Cross" in the Colosseum, where he was followed by thousands of pilgrims. On April 4 he wrote to his sister, Mrs. Rodrigue: —

"I do not like to describe, and I am sure you will not like to read, of the attentions that are paid to me by dukes, princes, cardinals, and marquises, and, I believe I mentioned before, by the Holy Father himself. These are as numerous and as distinguished as if I could trace back my genealogy to the fourteenth century."

Among these manifestations of honour he must have often thought with humility of the time when he worked as a day-labourer on the roadside in Pennsylvania.

On leaving Rome he intended to go to Spain to see the prime minister, O'Donnell, who had expressed a desire to meet him and learn the condition of the Spanish interests in the Antilles, concerning which the archbishop had many documents. But his health prevented him from going to Madrid. On June 25 he was at Aix-les-Bains in Savoy. Thence, after a short stay, he travelled through France and England to Ireland, where he was to preach at the laying of the corner-stone of the Catholic University in Dublin. This event took place on July 20. His text on the occasion was: "Woe to you, lawyers! for you have taken away the key of knowledge: you yourselves have not entered in, and those that were entering in you have hindered." (St. Luke xi. 52.) Wherever he travelled in Ireland crowds gathered to greet him. He disliked the English Government because of its attempt to help the Southern Rebellion; and he had also the natural antipathy of the Irishman for the oppressor of his religious faith and of his native land. In those days all the English parties were opposed to Ireland and to the United States. He made a strong, anti-English speech in the Dublin Rotundo before an immense audience. He spoke particularly of the resentment of Americans on account of English unfriendliness to their country in its hour of peril. "I tell you, gentlemen," said he, "that even if peace was restored to the whole country of America to-morrow, the people would scarcely unbelt themselves until they had put other questions to right. They feel sore; they feel that their national dignity has been attacked; that in the moment of their trial and difficulty, an ungenerous attack has been made on them, and they have unfortunately treasured up the memory of that attack with a feeling of revenge."

On July 31 we find him in the South of Ireland at Cork, where the people gave him a dinner. A few days later he sailed from Queenstown in the "Scotia," and reached New York on August 12. His clerical fellow-passengers on the steamer were Archbishops Wood, of Philadelphia, and Purcell, of Cincinnati; Bishop McCloskey, of Albany; the Rev. Dr. McNeirny, now bishop of Albany; the Rev. Henry A. Brann, D. D., the first priest of the American College at Rome; and the Rev. Joseph W. Stenger, of St. Sulpice, Paris, and now rector of the Catholic Church in Charleston, West Virginia. On the archbishop's arrival, the whole city turned out to greet him. The municipal authorities presented him with congratulatory addresses. After a few days' rest he went to Washington. There he was invited to dinner by Secretary Seward. The day fixed for the dinner was Friday, and the archbishop suggested that it was not a good day for a banquet. "Never mind," said the secretary, "I shall see that you will be provided for." When the very large and distinguished company met in the dining hall, there was no meat of any kind on the table. All were compelled to eat fish. The archbishop often said that this was the most delicate compliment ever paid to him. Mr. Lincoln's Government soon after intimated to the Holy See that it would be pleased if the archbishop, who had done so much for the country, should be raised to the dignity of cardinal. The matter was taken into consideration at Rome.

The sea voyage as usual had revived him. The Sunday after his return from Washington, he delivered a discourse before an immense crowd in the cathedral in Mott Street. Many of the people were tired of the war. There was much discontent at the expenses incurred by the Government, and at the failure of many of the generals to put down the rebellion. All longed for peace, and regretted the loss of life and treasure, and some were ready for any compromise that could be made with the South. But the archbishop in this discourse urged the people to finish the war at once by putting forth all their strength.

" If I had a voice in the councils of the country," he exclaimed, " I would say let volunteering continue; if the three hundred thousand on your list be not enough this week, next week make a draft of three hundred thousand more. It is not cruel, this. This is mercy; this is humanity. It is necessary to be true, to be patriotic, to do for the country what the country needs, and the blessing of God will recompense those who discharge their duty without faltering and without violating any of the laws of God or man."

This address was denounced by many of the archbishop's own flock, as well as by the " Copperheads" of the country, — a name given to friends of the South, living in the North, who favoured peace at any price. Complaints were sent to Rome against him, charging him with overstepping the boundaries of his sacred office. The "Courier des États Unis," the French organ in New York, was particularly severe on him. The archbishop answered his critics in the "Metropolitan Record;" and also made answer to them at Rome, through his friend, Rev. Dr. Bernard Smith, a learned Benedictine monk for years a professor of theology in the Propaganda College.

On December 15 he writes to Dr. Smith an account of the purchase of the new seminary of St. Joseph at Troy. The property cost sixty thousand dollars. In his letter to Dr. Smith, who was his agent with the Propaganda, the archbishop declares his intention of putting the seminary under the control of the Sulpicians, — a body of holy and learned priests organized by Father Olier in France, for the training of young men for the priesthood, — and speaks of the prosperity of the colleges under the Jesuit Fathers of his diocese. He tells also of the flourishing condition of the academies for girls under the charge of the Sisters of Charity, of the Sisters of Mercy, of the Ursuline nuns, of the Ladies of the Sacred Heart, and of other religious orders. He speaks of the well-established reformatories for boys and girls, and of the "House of the Good Shepherd" for fallen women, which had then one hundred and thirty inmates. He also describes the orphan asylums, and mentions a new one just founded for the Germans. He wanted the Propaganda to see that his devotion to the interests of his country had not interfered, as was charged, with the administration of his diocese; and he asked Dr. Smith to translate his letter into Italian, and present it to Cardinal Barnabo.

The founding of St. Joseph's Seminary at Troy, for the education of candidates for the priesthood, was the archbishop's last work. His health again broke down, and his strength was ebbing away; the end was fast approaching. He lived in Madison Avenue with his sister, Mrs. Rodrigue. Here he spent his time. Though he ceased to write for the newspapers, he read them as carefully as ever. Paintings pleased him; he had made a good collection of them during his visits to Europe. In 1857, while in Rome, the Pope and Cardinal Antonelli gave him several beautiful works of art, which he admired very much and showed with pleasure to visitors and strangers.

On Holy Thursday, April 2, 1863, nine months before his death, he said Mass for the last time. After that date, he often tried to say it, but weakness compelled him to give up the attempt. He was never a heavy eater, but now his appetite almost completely failed. He disliked to be consulted about his meals. Sometimes he would spend the whole day without eating anything but a light breakfast. He amused himself sometimes by playing billiards, on a table in his house, with an imaginary adversary. He then took to studying geography, and spent hours poring over the globes; or he applied himself to astronomy. His intellectual appetites seemed to grow with the decrease of bodily strength. It became for a time almost a passion with him to have his globes carried on a fine summer evening to the top of his stable, and there for hours to study the stars. His love for the Greek and Latin classics also returned with old age.

His last sermon was in June, 1863, at the dedication of St. Teresa's Church. In this discourse, his intense patriotism again showed itself. He urged on all the necessity of praying and working for the welfare of the country. "We must pray," said he. "I do not say for peace, which appears at this moment ridiculous, since there is only one that can give peace, and the other won't have it. We may pray the Almighty to bring matters to a conclusion. One side may make war, but it requires two to make peace."

In July he went to Baltimore to attend the funeral of Archbishop Kenrick, who had died very suddenly. A day or two after, the great draft-riots broke out in New York. For several days the city was at the mercy of a mob which robbed, murdered, and committed every kind of outrage. The governor of the State, Horatio Seymour, called on the archbishop to aid him in putting down the riots. The governor knew the great influence which the archbishop had over the New York populace, and so he wrote on July 14 to the aged prelate : —

"Will you exert your powerful influence to stop the disorders now reigning in this city? I do not wish to ask anything inconsistent with your sacred duties; but if you can with propriety aid the civil authorities at this crisis, I hope you will do so."

The archbishop was willing to do what he could, and so he issued an address to the rioters, inviting them to come and listen to him, as he was not able to go to them.

They did not come, however, for their leaders and the greater part of them were not members of the Catholic Church. But in their stead came several thousand of the poor and industrious labouring class, who were suffering from the effects of the war, and who were not able to purchase substitutes. He spoke to them in a feeble and broken voice, and advised them to go home and live in peace. They cheered him, promised to obey his words, and dispersed. This speech plainly showed that his mental vigour as well as his physical strength were fast going. In the following August and September he sought recreation by the sea-shore, but his health was not much benefited even by the sea air. Early in December he was compelled to take to his bed. He was not expected to live beyond Christmas. The doctors finally said that he could not recover. On December 29 his Vicar-General, Father Starrs, and his devoted secretary, Father McNeirny, told him what the physicians had said. When he heard it, his only words were, "Did they say so?" He was not afraid to die. He made his confession to the Rev. William Quinn, afterward Vicar-General of New York, who gave him the last sacraments, extreme unction, and holy communion. On Sunday, Jan. 3, 1864, the venerable Jesuit, Father McElroy, said Mass in the room of the dying archbishop. He died about seven o'clock on the evening of the same day. Bishop McCloskey, who afterward became his successor, was present at the last moment, and recited the prayers for the dying. The other principal persons in the room at the time were Bishop Loughlin, of Brooklyn, Vicar-General Starrs, and Father McNeirny, and the archbishop's two sisters. The funeral took place on January 7, the anniversary of his consecration. Eight bishops and several hundred priests attended the solemn requiem Mass celebrated on the occasion by the Right Rev. Bishop Timon, of Buffalo. Bishop McCloskey, of Albany, preached the funeral sermon.

Archbishop Hughes was a self-made man, one of a class for which our country is remarkable. Our institutions, which foster and develop individualism, putting no limit to the aspirations or the possibilities of natural ability or genius, are the nursing mother of men like Hughes, — men of grit, of courage, of talent, and of perseverance. He rose by sheer strength of character and natural genius from the lowest to the highest rank. Everything was against him when he landed on our shores. His race and religion were despised. He had very little education, no money, and no powerful friends. He began as a day-labourer in the fields and on the roadside. Almost without friends he succeeded; he persisted. He had formed a purpose and he would realize it. He studied; he prayed. With God and manly courage he conquered every difficulty. He had the faith, the valour, the irrepressibility, and the piety of the old Irish race. His piety led him into the sanctuary; but if he had not become a priest, there was material in him to make a great general, a great lawyer, a great politician, or a great statesman. If he had not become a bishop, he would have ranked in another career with other distinguished men of his race, with General Sheridan, Marshal Nugent, Count Taafe, O'Connell, O'Donnell, or O'Conor. He was physically as brave and as daring as the gallant soldier who made the wonderful ride down the Shenandoah valley. Had he lived in the Middle Ages he would have probably been made Pope, and ranked with Gregory VII. or Alexander III. He would never have yielded to the despotism of a king or to the violence of a mob.

The mob might kill him, but he would die with his face to the foe. He would not have been merely passive in a fight; his courage was active and aggressive. If the "Know-Nothings" had dared to carry out their threats, the archbishop himself would have planned and led the defence of his people and of his Church. He would never be found in the rear of a battle. With what a soldier's eye he followed the fights of the Civil War, and with what Napoleonic intuition he saw the strong and the weak points of the campaigns of our generals!

He had the diplomatic talent of a Richelieu. Secretary Seward, who was himself a clever statesman, recognizing his power and influence, saw in Archbishop Hughes an equal, if not a superior, to himself in the art of governing men. No one did more than the first Catholic archbishop of New York for our country in her hour of peril, by his influence both at home and abroad. Let us hope that some day our grateful citizens, remembering his patriotism, and all his services to his country, will erect to his memory a statue to perpetuate his fame. It should be erected near that of his friends, the great secretary of state, Seward, and the great war-president, Lincoln. Less worthy citizens have received this homage after their death.

But whatever our citizens or the State may do to

keep his memory green, the Catholic Church in America, and especially in New York, will never forget his invaluable services. He found her on the ground, despised and dejected. He lifted her up and made her respectable. She was looked upon as the despised sect of foreign immigrants; he made her respected and feared. How he fought, and how he despised, and how he struck those who assailed her! He freed her from the slavery of unprincipled laymen who intruded into the sanctuary and usurped ecclesiastical power. He crushed the schismatic and uncanonical "trustee system" with one blow of his strong crozier. He stood in front, like a giant, dealing death blows to prejudice and bigotry. He exposed them to public contempt and ridicule by his trenchant logic, his cutting sarcasm, and his clear statement of the truth. He fought for God, his Church, and his country. If he did not succeed in everything, his failures were few. He failed to secure the blessings of religious education for the children of the public schools. But his arguments in this cause live after him, and have never been answered.

He was a man both feared and loved; but no one hated or could hate him. Even those who feared him, admired him. He was so open, so just, so fair, so impartial, and so manly in his fight for what he thought right. I crossed the ocean with him in 1862. I was then a young priest, returning home from the

Eternal City. He was coming back after his mission to Europe, where he had done so much to keep France and England from recognizing the Southern Confederacy. I remember how he used to stand in the evening in some sheltered spot, surrounded by a group of passengers anxious to catch a word from his lips. Every one listened to him as to a chief, a leader, an oracle. He stood among the passengers like one born to command. He seemed the owner of the vessel, and he looked as if he could command the very waves. I remember how he defended our national Government from some who were criticising it; how warmly he praised our free institutions, showed the error of the Southern secession, and the necessity of sticking to the Union. His voice was clear, his manner quiet, but his words were forcible, and silenced the critic.

The free institutions of America were almost as dear to him as his Christian faith. Take him all in all he was not only the greatest prelate the Catholic Church in America has ever had; but he was as great and as good a citizen as ever deserved well of the American republic. Let her do him honor!

Deo et patriae.

INDEX.

A.

Adams, John Quincy, 108.
American College at Rome founded by Pius IX., 135.
"American, Native," party, 88.
Annaloghan, the place of his birth, 13.
Anti-Slavery Address of Irishmen, 155.
Antonelli, Cardinal, 162.
Apologia pro vita sua, 132.
Arath, Bishop of, 43.
Atlantic cable, the laying of, 135.
"Aurora," a newspaper, 90.

B.

Bangs, Dr., 75.
Bardstown, 27.
Barnabo, Cardinal, 132; letter to, 132; refuses resignation of Bishop Hughes, 134.
Bayley, Bishop, of Newark, 118.
Bedini, Monsignore, 118; is mobbed, 119.
Benton, Mr., 108.
Biddle, Mr., 115.
Bond, Dr., 75.
Brann, Rev. Henry A., 165.
Breckenridge, Dr., 48; controversy with, 49.
Brownson, Dr. O. A., 129, 155.
Bruté, Rev. Father, a sketch of his life, 27.
Butts, Major, 115.

C.

Calhoun, John C., 108.
Campbell, postmaster-general, 118.
Cathedral, building of the new, 135; building stopped for lack of funds, 136; Cardinal McCloskey completes the work, 136.
Catholic emancipation won in the year 1829, by O'Connell, 14.
Catholic political party, 81.
Catholic population of New York in 1838, 58.
"Catholic Vote, The," 125.
Cavour plots the overthrow of the Pope's territory, 136.
"Centinel, The Adams," a newspaper, 31.
Chambersburg, the home of John Hughes in the new world, 21.
Church Property Bill of 1855, 91.
"Church Register," an Episcopalian newspaper, 43.
Churches dedicated by Bishop Hughes, 133.
Clay, Henry, 126.
Coadjutor, Archbishop Hughes applies for, 134.

College, American, at Rome, founded, 135, 162.
"Commercial Advertiser," 99.
Controversy, *First*, with Rev. W. H. Delancey, an Episcopalian clergyman, 43; *Second*, exposing "The Protestant," 45; *Third*, "The Breckenridge," 51-53; with David Hale, 88; with "Kirwan," 100; with the "Tribune," 112; with General Cass, 120; with Erastus Brooks, 123; with "Equitas" 131; with "Courier des États Unis," 167.
"Controversy, School," 65; close of, 80; Governor Seward's sympathy, 81.
"Conversion and Edifying Death of Andrew Dunn" (a book written by Bishop Hughes), 38.
Conwell, Bishop, 32; makes an illegal surrender of his rights, 35.
"Copperheads," 166.
Corrigan, Michael A., attends the American College at Rome, 135; as Archbishop, completes the cathedral, 136.
Council of Baltimore, sixth, 101.
Council, first provincial, of New York in 1854, 122.
"Courier and Enquirer," 99.
"Crammer," 45.
Cummings, Rev. Dr., 129.

D.

Dayton American Minister, 160.
"Death, Ode to," a poem by Bishop Hughes, 144.
Debt of Church in New York in 1841, 88.
Delancey, Rev. W. H., 43.

Delaney, Col. Sharp, 115.
Deluol, Rev. Mr., 103.
De Smet, Father, 92.
Douglas, Stephen A., 108.
Dubois, Rev. John, sketch of his life, 25.
"Dunn, Andrew," 39.

E.

Eccleston, Archbishop, 63.
Emancipation proclamation, 151.
"Equitas" attacks Bishop Hughes, 130; Bishop Hughes's answer to, 131.
Eugénie, Empress, 161.

F.

Flaget, first bishop of Bardstown, 27.
Fordham, 101.
"Franklin Repository," a newspaper, 28.
"Freeman's Journal," The, 106.
Frenaye, Mr., a friend of Father Hughes, 47.

G.

Galitzin, Father, a Russian Prince, 46.
Galitzin, Madame, first superioress of the Manhattanville Academy, 87.
Gavazzi, an apostate priest, 120.
George IV. signs bill of Catholic emancipation, 42.
Greeley Horace, 114.

H.

Henry IV., 39.
Herald, 99.

Herald, Catholic, 40.
Heyden, Father, 36.
Hill, Rose, 86.
Hogan, an unworthy priest, 35.
"Home of my Fathers," a poem, 142.
Hughes, John, works as a laborer at Emmittsburg, 24; obtains work as a gardener at Mount Saint Mary's, 26; enters the college in 1820, 26; he teaches at Mount Saint Mary's, 27; his first controversy, 28; gaining a reputation as an orator, 30; cultivates poetry, 31; ordained priest, 32; made pastor of Saint Joseph's Church, 36; converts to the Catholic Church through the means of the sermons of Father Hughes, 40; charities founded by him, 40; appointed coadjutor to the Bishop of New York, 56; establishes a theological seminary, 59; goes to Europe, visits the Leopoldine Society of Austria, receives a large donation for his new seminary of Saint John's at Fordham, 66; meets Daniel O'Connell and speaks from the same platform with him, 66; great speech on school question, 75; life menaced, 81; speech at Carroll Hall, 81; forms a Catholic party, 81; opposed by the politicians, 83; wonderful activity, 91; financial plans, 91; anecdote, 92; cows the "Native American" mobs, 95; compels Mayor Harper to do his duty, 98; threat to assassinate him, 98; attacks the "New York Herald" and the "Commercial Advertiser," 99; patriotism, 99; visits Europe, 100; sympathy with Irish patriots, 104, 105; attacks D'Arcy McGee and the "Young Ireland" faction, 106; defends the temporal power of the Pope, 107; daily labor described, 110, 111; is made an Archbishop, 112; attacks Kossuth, 114; ousts the trustees of Saint Peter's Church, 116; confidence in his popularity, 120; controversy with Erastus Brooks, 124; is charged with being a politician, 125; only vote for Henry Clay, 126; hard work from 1855 to 1858, 127; visits Newfoundland, 127; health gives way, 128; lectures in Baltimore and Pittsburgh, 128; attacks on, 130; Cardinal Barnabo refuses his resignation, 134; asks for a coadjutor, 134; pastoral letter on the temporal power of the Pope, 137; makes a trip to the South, travels to St. Augustine, Florida, 138; letter to Charles O'Conor, 138; replies to his critics on temporal power, 139; sermon on the temporal power, 139; a Southern newspaper describes his style of preaching, 140; poems, 142; description of a storm at sea, 149; patriotism, 154; opposition to negro slavery, 154; assists the government during the Civil War, 158; goes to Europe to help the government, 160; interviews Napoleon III., 160; last sermon, 169; speech to the mob, 170; last sickness and death, 170, 171; character, 171, *et seq.*

I.

"Immaculate Conception," Church of, 133.

INDEX

Intriguers, Sardinian, against the Holy See, 139.
Ireland, condition of, in 1840, 66.
Irish soldiers in our Revolutionary War, 115.

J.

Journal of Commerce, 90.
"Jubilee of American Freedom," 148.

K.

Keating, Col., 115.
Kenney, Rev., a Jesuit father, 54.
Kenrick, Bishop, sketch, 43.
Ketchum, Hiram, 75.
"Kirwan," 100; unmasked, 109.
Know-Nothing party, 99.
Knox, Dr., 75.
Kossuth, 114.

L.

Lafargeville, 59.
Levins, Rev. Thomas C., 44.
Limerick, Treaty of, 19.
Lincoln, President, 157.
Loco-foco party, 85.
Loughlin, Bishop, of Brooklyn, 118.
Lynch, Bishop, of Charleston, 138, 156.

M.

Martyrs, Japanese, 162.
Mary Angela, Sister, 44
Maryland, 23.
Mason, 159.
Matthew, Rev. Father, 154.

Matthews, Very Rev. Father, 43.
McCloskey, Cardinal, completed the work on the cathedral, 136.
McElroy, Father, S. J., 171.
McGee, Thomas D'Arcy, 106.
McNally, Bishop, of Clogher, Ireland, 133; letter to, 133.
McNeirny, Rev. Francis, 123, 160.
Melanchthon, 39.
"Metropolitan Record," Archbishop Hughes replies to his critics on the temporal power, 139.
Metternich, 66.
Mexico, a proposed visit to, 54.
Mob, "Native American," 95.
Mobs, "Know-Nothing," 122.
Mount Saint Mary, description, 24; the college burned down in 1824, Mr. Hughes collecting funds for a new college, the new college built in 1826, 31.
Moylan, Stephen, 115.
Mulledy, Rev. Father, a Jesuit, 55.
Mulloch, Bishop, 127.
Murray, Rev. Nicholas, 109.

N.

Napoleon III., 160.
"Nation," The New York, 106.
Nugent, Marshal, 66.

O.

O'Connell, Daniel, 14, 154.
O'Conor, Charles, a distinguished lawyer, Bishop Hughes writes to him on the Pope's temporal power, 138.
O'Donnell, Spanish statesman, 163.
Orangemen, 18.
Oxford, New York, 91.,

INDEX. 181

P.

Penal laws, description of some of them, 15; a story told by John Hughes concerning them, 18.
Pius IX., founds the American College at Rome, 135; letter to the Bishops of the United States in 1855, 135.
Poems, 142.
Politics and religion, 71.
Population, Catholic, in New York in 1838, 58.
Power, Rev. Dr., 47.
Preaching, his style described, 140.
Press, Propaganda, publishes Bishop Hughes's pastoral letter on the temporal power, 138.
"Press, The Catholic," article in "The Metropolitan Record," 30.
Preston, Rev. Thomas S., 123.
"Protestant," a newspaper, 44.
Public School Society, remonstrance of, 75, 134.

Q.

Quinn, Rev. William, 171.

R.

Reese, Dr., 75.
Ribbonmen, a secret organization, their character, 14.
Richelieu, Cardinal, 173.
Richmond, 157.
Rodrigue, Mrs., letter to, 163.
"Roman Question," The, becomes unusually interesting, 136.

S.

School question, 67; Bishop Hughes addresses the Public School Society on the, 68; petition to the Common Council for a share of the school fund rejected, 71; an address of the Roman Catholics to the fellow-citizens on the, 72, 73; The Public School Society strongly opposes the bishop's efforts, 75; the Protestant churches oppose and attack the Catholic petition, 76; brought before the Senate at Albany, 78; the Press helped the Public School Society, 79.
Sedgwick, Theodore, 75.
Seton, Mother, 103.
Seward, sympathy with Bishop Hughes, 81; advocates denominational schools, 85; his message to the legislature in 1842, 85, 157.
Seymour, Horatio, 169.
Sisters of Charity, 100.
"Slave, The," a poem, 142.
Slavery, negro, opposed by Bishop Hughes, 154.
Slidell, 159.
Smith, Dr., 168.
"Soft-Shell" democrats, 125.
Spring, Dr., 75.
Stenger, Rev. Joseph W., 165.
St. John's Orphan Asylum, 40.
St. Joseph's Church, New York, 91.
St. Louis' Church, Buffalo, 90.
St. Michael's Church, Philadelphia, 95.
St. Peter's debt, 116.
Synod, first, in New York, 89.

T.

Temporal power of the Pope, 107, 108; plotting against the, 136.
Teresa, Church of St., 169.
Thouvenel, French statesman, 160.

Timon, Bishop, 90.
Tract society, Father Hughes tries to found, 38.
Tracy, Father, 133.
Trustee system, 34; letter of Father Hughes to Father Bruté on the, 36; Bishop Conwell makes an illegal surrender to the trustees, 37; flourishes in New York, 59; conflict between the trustees and Father Hughes, 60, *et seq.*
Trustees of St. Mary's Church make trouble, Father Hughes builds a new church, calls it St. John's and thus he completely conquers the trustees, 47.
Trustees of St. Peter's mismanage the property, 116.

U.

Umiltà, ancient convent of, purchased by the Pope for the American College, 135.
United States, Irishmen eager to become citizens of, 22; refuses to interfere with ecclesiastical jurisdiction, 37.
University, Catholic, of Dublin, 164.

V.

Vauxhall garden, 105.
Victor Emmanuel, King, 136.
Vincennes, 27.

W.

Weed, Thurlow, 92.
Wood, Archbishop, 165.

X.

Xavier, Francis, St., 162.

Y.

"Young Ireland," 129.

MAKERS OF AMERICA.

The following is a list of the subjects and authors so far arranged for in this series. The volumes will be published at the uniform price of $1.00, and will appear in rapid succession: —

Christopher Columbus (1436-1506), and the Discovery of the New World. By CHARLES KENDALL ADAMS, President of Cornell University.

John Winthrop (1588-1649), First Governor of the Massachusetts Colony. By Rev. JOSEPH H. TWICHELL.

Robert Morris (1734-1806), Superintendent of Finance under the Continental Congress. By Prof. WILLIAM G. SUMNER, of Yale University.

James Edward Oglethorpe (1689-1785), and the Founding of the Georgia Colony. By HENRY BRUCE, Esq.

John Hughes, D.D. (1797-1864), First Archbishop of New-York: a Representative American Catholic. By HENRY A. BRANN, D.D.

Robert Fulton (1765-1815): His Life and its Results. By Prof. R. H. THURSTON, of Cornell University.

Francis Higginson (1587-1630), Puritan, Author of "New England's Plantation," etc. By THOMAS W. HIGGINSON.

Peter Stuyvesant (1602-1682), and the Dutch Settlement of New-York. By BAYARD TUCKERMAN, Esq., author of a "Life of General Lafayette," editor of the "Diary of Philip Hone," etc., etc.

Thomas Hooker (1586-1647), Theologian, Founder of the Hartford Colony. By GEORGE L. WALKER, D.D.

Charles Sumner (1811-1874), Statesman. By ANNA L. DAWES.

Thomas Jefferson (1743-1826), Third President of the United States. By JAMES SCHOULER, Esq., author of "A History of the United States under the Constitution."

William White (1748-1836), Chaplain of the Continental Congress, Bishop of Pennsylvania, President of the Convention to organize the Protestant Episcopal Church in America. By Rev. JULIUS H. WARD, with an Introduction by Right Rev. Henry C. Potter, D.D., Bishop of New-York.

Jean Baptiste Lemoine, *sieur* de Bienville (1680-1768), French Governor of Louisiana, Founder of New Orleans. By GRACE KING, author of "Monsieur Motte."

Alexander Hamilton (1757-1804), Statesman, Financier, Secretary of the Treasury. By Prof. WILLIAM G. SUMNER, of Yale University.

Father Juniper Serra (1713-1784), and the Franciscan Missions in California. By JOHN GILMARY SHEA, LL.D.

Cotton Mather (1663-1728), Theologian, Author, Believer in Witchcraft and the Supernatural. By Prof. BARRETT WENDELL, of Harvard University.

Robert Cavelier, *sieur* de La Salle (1643-1687), Explorer of the Northwest and the Mississippi. By EDWARD G. MASON, Esq., President of the Historical Society of Chicago, author of "Illinois" in the Commonwealth Series.

Thomas Nelson (1738-1789), Governor of Virginia, General in the Revolutionary Army. Embracing a Picture of Virginian Colonial Life. By THOMAS NELSON PAGE, author of "Mars Chan," and other popular stories.

George and Cecilius Calvert, Barons Baltimore of Baltimore (1605-1676), and the Founding of the Maryland Colony. By WILLIAM HAND BROWNE, editor of "The Archives of Maryland."

Sir William Johnson (1715-1774), and The Six Nations. By WILLIAM ELLIOT GRIFFIS, D.D., author of "The Mikado's Empire," etc., etc.

Sam. Houston (1793-1862), and the Annexation of Texas. By HENRY BRUCE, Esq.

Joseph Henry, LL.D. (1797-1878), Savant and Natural Philosopher. By FREDERIC H BETTS, Esq.

Ralph Waldo Emerson. By Prof. HERMAN GRIMM, author of "The Life of Michael Angelo," "The Life and Times of Goethe," etc.

DODD, MEAD, & COMPANY,
753 and 755 Broadway, New York.

www.ingramcontent.com/pod-product-compliance
Lightning Source LLC
Chambersburg PA
CBHW031444160426
43195CB00010BB/841